Long-Distance

Grandparenting

Connecting with Your Grandchildren from Afar

Long-Distance

Grandparenting

Connecting with Your Grandchildren from Afar

Willma Willis Gore

Sanger, California

Printed in the United States of America.

Published by
Quill Driver Books/Word Dancer Press, Inc.,
1254 Commerce Way, Sanger, CA 93657
559-876-2170 / 800-497-4909
QuillDriverBooks.com

Quill Driver Books/Word Dancer Press books may be purchased for educational, fund-raising, business or promotional use. Please contact Special Markets, Quill Driver Books/Word Dancer Press, Inc. at the above address or phone numbers.

Quill Driver Books/Word Dancer Press Project Cadre:
Doris Hall, Stephen Blake Mettee, Carlos Olivas, Cassandra Williams

First Printing

ISBN 1-884956-75-0 • 978-1884956-75-1

**To order a copy of this book, please call
1-800-497-4909.**

Library of Congress Cataloging-in-Publication Data

Gore, Willma Willis.
  Long-distance grandparenting : connecting with your grandchildren from afar / by Willma Willis Gore.
    p. cm.
ISBN-13: 978-1-884956-75-1 (trade pbk.)
ISBN-10: 1-884956-75-0 (trade pbk.)
1. Grandparenting. 2. Long-distance relationships. 3. Grandparent and child. I. Title.
HQ759.9.G666 2007
306.874'5–dc22

                                                          2007036661

This book is dedicated to Esther Ann Chrysler Tate, my long-deceased grandmother, and to all grandparents who, like her, inspire their grandchildren to reach for the stars.

Contents

Acknowledgments

Besides my own observations and grandparenting experience, this book contains the wit and wisdom contributed by more than sixty people, from Maine to California, Washington State to Florida. My sincere thanks to them and grandparents referred to me by friends and relatives. Thanks also to my ever-supportive writer colleagues in Arizona and California with special recognition for Anne Crosman for her astute review of the manuscript.

To protect sometimes fragile relationships and because I asked contributors to speak with unbridled honesty, no real names or locations of the contributors have been used in this book; however, all who have contributed wit and wisdom are listed alphabetically in the "Contributors" section on page 91.

Lastly, my appreciation to Steve Mettee, publisher of Quill Driver Books. His faith in me launched the rewarding experience of researching and writing this book.

Wit & Wisdom–from Long-Distance Grandparenting

Long ago, grandparents often lived as close to their grandchildren as the back porch rocking chair. Many grandparents were down the block, across a field or over the garden fence from their grandkids.

My maternal grandmother, Esther Tate, was a "live-in" grandparent for four months of the year. She also spent another four months with one set of cousins, yet another four with a third set. She was my fountain of wisdom, a voracious reader who shared all manner of facts and philosophies with me. My mother and father gave me love and support but Grandmother was the one who had time to sit and talk. She made me feel that time with me was worthwhile.

In today's mobile society, effective, rewarding grand-parenting is a challenge for everyone–for parents, grandparents and grandkids. Miles–even whole countries–separate many of us from our grandchildren. What's a grandparent to do?

"Whatever it takes," says long-time grandmother Naomi, who reels off a list: "letters, long-distance telephone, e-mail, air, rail, or road trips. Countless options are available." Naomi lives in Arizona. One grandchild, a college sophomore, called her last week from the East Coast to talk about career choices.

I had hoped to duplicate with my grandchildren the rocking-chair closeness I knew with my grandmother, but circumstances have made me a long-distance grandparent. And so I have been forced to seek out and share whatever it takes to be with them for specific occasions even though physically far away most of the time.

"When hosting a grandkid adventure," says Arlene of Citrus Heights, California, "take one child at a time. Be sure the kid is old enough to enjoy and learn from the adventure." She has four grandchildren—all long distance. She took her eldest, a boy, on a trip to New York, then to Israel, Jordan, and China. Another time she took one girl to Hawaii where they rented a jeep and explored the island.

Arlene took yet another girl who starred on her high school basketball team to the Olympics in Australia. They watched the U.S. girls win a gold medal in basketball. The fourth girl she took to the Galapagos and Quito, Peru.

"Hosting them one at a time gave each child my undivided attention for the trip, and it was as much fun for me as for them." (See Chapter 10 and the Resources section at the back of this book for commercial trips specially designed for several generations.)

What if finances of either parents or grandparents do not allow for long distance travel or sponsored tours?

Sedona, Arizona, grandparent, Lois, hosts her grandkids during spring breaks from school. Their working parents can't take time from jobs but pay train fare for Kristen and Karl. Besides hikes among the beautiful red rocks of the area, kids and grandma lie on the lawn at night and star-gaze. An amateur astronomer, Lois identifies the constellations and recites myths and sky-lore. This is a treat for the grandkids, as the night sky is rarely visible from the children's home in Los Angeles. The only stars in their experience are seen in the movies. Sedona's skies are clear an average of 350 days of the year. Because outdoor street lighting is not allowed, ambient light does not interfere with star-gazing. "There're too many stars to count even if I stayed here all night," exclaimed awe-struck grandson, Karl.

Anecdotes and advice in this book are based on interviews and written reports from dozens of grandparents and grandchildren across the U.S. All grandparenting experiences are not created equal. Grandparents sometimes become rivals. Money can be scarce. Time and transportation can be problems. Schedules conflict.

This book offers examples of ways grandparents, parents, and grandchildren have connected and profited in spite of the distances among them. You may adopt some ideas and discard others, as you should, because whatever you do, your style will be uniquely your own, as it should be.

Happy grandparenting!

Chapter 1

Setting the Time and Place

Years ago, when my new husband and I mentioned to my teen-age sister how much she would enjoy spending a part of her vacation with her grandmother in a mountain cabin, we got a sharp retort.

"Going to Gram's may be all right for you two, but you're married. You've lived your lives."

Consult all Parties Involved

If the children are preteen, grandparent visiting time should be set by the parents in consultation with the grandparents.

A family conference by phone or e-mail with grandparents is in order. Quite often, especially if Gram and Gramp live at a great distance, prospects of an airplane flight or train trip add to the attraction of the visit.

Grandparents usually have more free time than parents, as they may be retired or at least not on the career-building track, and the welcome mat is likely to be out at most any time for the grandkids. But grandparents, too, have schedules. Some may have booked a flight or cruise, paid for well in advance. Their availability may be as inflexible as dad's or mom's prescribed vacation days.

Older children, who have formed close ties with school friends, may prefer to spend vacation time with those friends. Even young teens will have their own ideas about timing, distance from home, and desire to visit Gram and Gramps.

"But Mom," protested Katie, "Judy's birthday is on July fifteenth. I don't care if Dad can't change his days off. I can't be away then." For this case, grandparents Marjory and Fred, 400 miles away, came to the rescue. After consulting Katie's parents, they invited granddaughter *and* Judy to visit together.

"This worked out well," says Marjory. "We were somewhat overwhelmed with the prospect of providing hour-by-hour entertainment for a teenage grandchild. In being together, the girls entertained each other as they decided which of our offerings they wanted to take in. They enjoyed sharing their comments about what they had seen and done.

"We purchased trip diaries for both girls and encouraged them to record and date their adventures. I helped the girls make Judy's birthday cake for her July fifteenth celebration. She'd been promised another celebration with other friends at the end of July when she returned home. We received a warm thank you from Judy's parents. And the girls want to come together again next year."

When Good Plans Go Awry

Connie, a single grandparent, divides her time between her children and their families in Toronto and her winter home the Phoenix. She always had a loving relationship with Melissa, her preteen Toronto granddaughter. Connie had not been back to Toronto for a year when the girl turned thirteen. She sent the airfare for a flight to Phoenix as a gift to the girl to celebrate her arrival into her teens.

Connie spent hours planning Melissa's visit. She lined up scenic outings, art shows, musical and drama events. She felt sure Melissa would enjoy them. On arrival day, panic set in as Connie waited in the debarking area. No Melissa. On closer inspection she saw a slender figure wearing frayed jeans, a black hat pulled low over a sullen face. Long, unkempt hair hung to the girl's shoulders. Yes, it was Melissa. There went Connie's memory of the girl at eleven who was always immaculately groomed and cheerful.

In spite of her surprise, Connie embraced the girl warmly. Melissa's words were, "Hello, Connie," as though her grandmother were a stranger. Not the old, "Hi, Grammy," and a return hug.

The vacation week turned into a nightmare–for Connie. Nothing she did or said elicited the least bit of enthusiasm from Melissa. Finally, the miserable ten days ended and she put Melissa back on the plane for her return home. There was no thank you from the girl. Two days later she received an e-mail from Melissa.. "Dear Grammy, I had such a wonderful time. Thank you. I hope I can come again. Love and hugs, Melly."

"Go figure," says Connie.

Trial and Error

Serena and second husband Vern are each parents of two grown children and grandparents to six grandkids. All live fairly near each other in Colorado.

The grandparents had moved away from their children and grandkids to the Tucson area where the elevation was better for Vern's health. An outgoing couple, they built a new home in a lovely residential community. They enjoyed life there and made many new friends in their age group. However, they greatly missed seeing their children and being in closer touch as the grandkids grew. Vern's health improved and they felt they could safely return to Colorado and their families. Instead of purchasing a home right away, they rented an apartment pending finding the right place.

The first year back, they discovered that being close to the families was not what they expected. Their children spent most of their free time with their friends and the teenaged grandkids had so many irons in the fire with school and sports that the grandparents' dream of dinners every Sunday with all the family gathered at the table simply did not come to pass. They saw two of the grandkids quite often—the three- and five-year-olds.

"Who can be better sitters than loving grandparents?" says Serena, with sarcasm in her voice.

She and Vern have now given notice on the rental and will soon move back to the community where they had been so happy with friends their own ages. "They think and play more like we do," says Vern.

Serena adds, "We had to test our emotions and skills in planning and see past our dreams into reality. It will be great to potluck again and visit with friends our age and share mutual loves and concerns."

Provide Options

As with most quandaries, good communication is the key. Grandchildren may not have the slightest idea what will occur on a visit. Talking over options with them in advance can be rewarding.

"My fourteen-year-old granddaughter from Virginia had a good time with me two years ago, here in Oregon," says Gretchen. "But last year she seemed reluctant to come. I couldn't get an explanation from her or from her parents. When I offered the chance for her to join me at an Elderhostel Intergenerational program at a mountain resort, she agreed to come. It was a learning experience for both of us. The optional offerings were educational and filled with activities for both young and old. She wants to do it again and I plan to do the same with her brother when he is a little older."

How Many at a Time?

"Give me one at a time," says Clarissa, a single grandmother who lives in Washington, D.C. "With one, we can make a choice between the Smithsonian and the National Museum of Art. With two preteens, I couldn't satisfy both in the amount of time we have.

"I don't mind having all three at once," says Marian. "But, if they're going to fight in my house like they fight at home, I want a 'smaller dose' at a time. My son's daughter and my daughter's daughter—cousins—get along much better than they get along with their siblings. I'm glad to have the two cousins together. They seem to be happy to be away from their brothers and sisters and have a fabulous time here with us."

"Two is usually better than three," says Phyllis. "With three, one is always the 'odd man out.'"

"Send all five," says Nadine, "I love them to pieces. When they quarrel, I order them to sit in chairs in a circle. I set the timer and make them sit and stare at each other for a half hour. Usually within in five minutes they are falling off the chairs in giggling fits."

Different Strokes for Different Folks

Many different attitudes and experiences exist in the grandparenting milieu. No one method is appropriate for all. "There are answers to all the questions about grandparenting—long or short distance," says Norma. "Talk to everybody involved and love will find the way."

Faith's story is a good example. "Four of my five children are boys. They are happily married to lovely women and live 200 to 800 miles away. I have had to face the fact that all my beautiful grandchildren's mothers have their own mothers to call upon for comfort, advice, questions, and just simply to share special moments. I don't interfere with their relationships, but it does often make for situations where I feel a little left out—as a mother and as a grandmother. The sons call to talk to their father, my husband, mostly about business. 'You and Mom take care' is often the closing from a son. They do not ask to speak to me.

"I have tried very hard to be low-key, not to interfere or make demands of anyone. Recently, I was surprised to learn that one daughter-in-law wants us be more involved in her life. The others seem not to care if I ever make my presence known, except, of course, for birthdays and Christmas, and those dates are for the grandchildren. Another has issues with her birth mother and has opened her arms to me while she tries desperately to have a good familial relationship on toxic ground. I encourage her to love, forgive, set boundaries, stand on her own feet, and allow her family their journey while she moves forward in hers. I also realize that this is good instruction for me to live by, as well!"

Chapter 2

Rules for Grandparents, Parents, and Grandkids

Although vacation time is meant to be a happy time for everybody–parents, grandparents and grandkids–it can't be allowed to be a free-for-all period when "anything the kid wants to do is okay."

Home Rules vs. Visiting Rules

Grandmother Isabel had some explaining to do when her daughter called and complained. Apparently grandson, Cliff's visit had opened a can of worms.

"Grandma let me do it," he shot back when his mother would not let him walk alone in the city to his friend's house three blocks away.

Isabel got on the phone with Cliff. "When you're here in the country, it is safe for you to go to the store by yourself. Remember that when you went to the grocery from our house, Granddad and I stood at the top of the driveway and watched you all the way. Walking alone isn't that safe in the city where you live."

Bedtime hours, special foods, allergies, medications, what do in emergencies, and TV and computer restrictions are a few of the essentials that parents and grandparents must agree on.

Two of Larry and Kate's grandchildren have severe allergies that plague them during visits to their grandparents' home in New Mexico. So now, Larry, Kate, and the family of three children and eight grandchildren rent cottages at Mono Lake at the foot of California's High Sierra. They canoe among the tuffa towers (mineral accumulations that have formed fascinating shapes near the shores of the lake). They fish in streams and high lakes in the surrounding mountains and set aside at least one day to visit the ghost town of Bodie where Grandpa Larry delights in spinning tales of the Old West. It has become an annual outing and very popular. At the close of each vacation, they set dates and make the reservations for the following year.

✓ A Different Kind of Holiday Sharing

Holidays are traditionally the time for all-generation get-togethers. "But, too many kids and grandkids under one roof on Christmas Eve and Christmas Day bring crises and chaos," say Robert and Beth.

These grandparents live 400 to 600 miles from their children so they stay home alone and send small gifts and blessings in time for the big day. "We encourage our sons and daughters-in-law, our daughters and sons-in-law, and their kids to spend Christmas together or individually—however they wish—but leave us grandparents out of it."

Instead, every year for the past five years, the grandparents' major gift to the entire brood is to rent a large home on the southern California coast for the week between Christmas and New Year. The grandkids bring their sleeping bags. The adults use beds or inflatable mattresses. The place has two refrigerators and everybody contributes food and beverages. Some come for the whole week; others for a few days.

"Beth posts a work list of those responsible for cooking meals, washing dishes, making coffee and—the coveted post—neat-room-checkers. The neat-room checker for each day is a secret person. The winner of the neatest room each day gets a package of M&Ms," says Robert.

"We now have a peaceful holiday vacation with the whole family. The beach is warm enough for building sand castles if not for swimming. These times have turned out to be perfect family reunions. Everybody is mellow and relaxed, nothing like the pre-Christmas rush."

Setting boundaries for when and how the holiday visits will transpire have kept Robert and Beth sane while pleasing everyone in the family.

Giving at Thanksgiving

For the last fifteen years, Janice and Jeremy, their three children and six grandchildren have held a Thanksgiving reunion at the grandparents' home or at the home of one of the children, 200 to 500 miles distant. At the close of each Thanksgiving day, the host for the next holiday volunteers.

"There's no special order and no counting of turns," says Janice. "Sometimes when last minute emergency makes it impossible for one of the kids to host, we just tell them to come here. Everybody helps with food and desserts and it is not a big burden for anyone."

Jeremy died last year and since then Janice plans to visit each family two or three times a year. "Except for the big annual reunion, I enjoy them in 'smaller doses.'"

One granddaughter has recently moved within 100 miles of Janice. "We talk on the phone or e-mail often. She has taken a new job and is in process of finding a home in her new community.

"During the time when I was teaching at a preschool, my son and his wife gave their three- and five-year-olds the option of staying with grandma or traveling to Canada with the parents. The boy chose to go with the parents but little Katie, then three, chose me. I took her to preschool every day and she was the happiest kid in the class.

"One set of my grandchildren's grandparents, the parents of one of my daughter-in-laws, does not visit the grandchildren but welcomes them whenever they come. They have set aside a room in their lovely large home that is just for the grandkids. They have equipped it with enough toys to stock a branch of Toys R Us," Janice reports. "I can't do that. I'd rather go to visit them."

Plans Subject to Change

"Our grandkids are not always brought up the way we wish they were," says Joan. "Even though we reared their parents 'right,' of course, we sometimes have to realize that teachings can slip out of synch between the apron strings and the marriage ties."

Joan's grandson Frank arrived at the Flagstaff Greyhound station after a day-long trip from Orange County, California. Joan's prior visits with Frank and his baby sister had always been at her daughter's home. This was to be the boy's first visit to what Joan called the countryside—the "boonies," in her city daughter's parlance.

Ten-year-old Frank embraced his grandmother warmly and talked nonstop of his wonderful bus trip, the man one seat ahead who let Frank watch him work on his laptop, and the nice lady who gave him a doughnut. On entering Joan's home in Payson, Frank instantly found the refrigerator and began to investigate the cheese and cold meat bin. He took the milk carton from the shelf and drank from it before Joan could stop him.

"Dad does it," Frank protested, when Joan took the carton away from him.

"Maybe Dad does it in your house, but this is my house and we pour the milk into a glass. I'll make sandwiches for lunch. We will take them out to the gazebo and sit at the table to eat while we watch the birds. Maybe the quail will come into the back yard."

"Can we shoot them?"

"Why in the world would we shoot them?"

"Dad said he'll take me quail hunting when I get bigger."

"We don't shoot our quail. We feed them."

Joan shelved her original plan–to take Frank swimming in a nearby lake and to the children's reading hour at the library. She decided instead to teach him how to put grain into her bird feeders, and syrup in the bottles for the hummingbirds. She helped him identify birds and took him on a hike where, in answer to her prayer, they caught glimpses through the trees of Old Bill, a part-time resident elk.

"Frank was fascinated with 'talking' to a raven that spent a lot of time in one of my trees," said Joan. She sent him away with a *Peterson's Guide* for reading about birds on his bus trip home.

Fighting Fire with Fire

Marge and Mark couldn't wait to host their two granddaughters in Anaheim and take them to visit California's Disneyland over the Fourth of July holiday. Their daughter, Pat, and her husband, who live in Boise, Idaho, had never allowed the girls, eight and ten, to have firecrackers or even sparklers. The only fireworks the girls had ever seen were in TV ads. As a child, Pat had been terrified when a neighborhood boy threw a lighted firecracker that exploded at her feet. She later conveyed fear of fire and explosions to her daughters.

The grandparents did not want to disobey their daughter's rules, so they devised a plan to "fight fire with fire," based on something they'd done years earlier with Pat's brothers. Marge and Mark had sat the boys down with candles in holders and matches to light the candles. They showed the boys how to quickly pass fingers over the flame to learn how hot it was. Then Mark took his sons to the fireplace to show them how fast paper caught fire even when it was a foot or more from the flame. Pat did not have this experience because she was much older and away at school at the time.

To present the granddaughters with some "fire experience," Marge repeated the experiment from long ago. The girls were fascinated and, like their uncles, long before, got a feel for flame and its discomforts. Grandma then presented them with a set of pretty candle holders to take home. They proudly showed them to their mother.

"We always felt that knowledge is safer than curiosity, and most kids are fascinated with fire," says Mark.

The trip to the Disneyland fireworks was an unforgettable event for the girls. When Marge and her daughter talked by phone about fire and the candle experiment, Pat agreed that it was time the girls knew how to strike a match, light a candle and—"use the candle snuffer."

When Relationships Threaten to Go up in Smoke

Bruce and Betty live 100 miles from their only grandchildren. They've always had a "best friends" relationship with their daughter, Barbara, her husband, and the three grandchildren—a girl now ten and two boys, eight and four.

Devoted as they are, Bruce and Betty have never been "hovering" grandparents. But they are always on-call for sitter service at Barbara's home and/or at their own large home. They still live in the house where they raised their own children. It has a large yard and a swimming pool. The grandkids love to visit.

Both Bruce and Betty are life-long smokers but never smoke in the daughter's non-smoking home. However, they used to smoke when the grandkids came to visit or rode in the car with them.

Daughter Barbara was not happy with the children being in the grandparents' smoke-contaminated home or car. This became a big problem when one grandson evidenced respiratory problems. Finally Barbara and her husband laid down the law. It was a tearful exchange on all sides, but Barbara insisted that, in consideration of the children's health, they could not be left in the care of the grandparents as long as Bruce and Betty smoked in the home or in the car.

Smokers may not realize it, but the odor and contamination linger even when cigarettes are not smoked nearby. Barbara tells us that all clothing in the children's backpacks or suitcases had to be laundered when they arrived home, even though grandmother had always laundered them before the kids left for home.

They hit on a compromise. The grandparents acceded to

Barbara's wishes, and now, whether or not the grandkids are expected or actually visiting, Bob and Betty smoke only outdoors. Their house has a pleasant odor. It's a matter of mutual trust and love and the resulting improvement in the grandparents' health is an additional plus.

Money "Talks" Grandma's Language

From time to time, Grandmother Catherine hosts three children from one son's family in her Lompoc, California, home. Catherine is not an enthusiastic cook so she often takes the children out to dinner. She was troubled by the kids' ordering a large meal but leaving half of it uneaten. She solved the problem by providing each with a ten-dollar-budget for dinner. They didn't have to eat it all, but had to take the leftovers home and eat them for breakfast the next morning. Each could keep any part of the ten dollars that he didn't spend on the meal. When this idea took hold, the kids vied with each other in getting the best meal for the least amount of money.

Catherine further challenged them by offering a reward of a shopping trip to buy gifts to take home to their parents. They could save part of their dining-out money if they chose. The children rose to the challenge and competed as to who could set aside the most.

The "Two Time Teller" Grandma

Grandmother Paula met a rather unusual situation that included house-sitting for her brother and his wife for ten days and caring for her eleven-year-old grandson, from a different branch of the family. Young Tom had never visited this home, and a host of new gadgets and experiences awaited him.

"I had to watch him all the time," says Paula. "The fancy recliner in front of her brother's TV had a handle that Tom operated as though he were shifting gears in a ten-ton truck. I had to ban him from sitting in the recliner for fear that his rough 'shifting of the gear' would ruin the mechanism."

The swimming pool had an automatic flushing system that Paula did not know how to operate. Brother had told her that nothing needed to be done in the short time he was away. The housing for all the pool apparatus contained knobs and levers galore. Tom wanted to explore. Paula forbade him to go near the pool house.

"Apparently, I turned my back too long," she says. "When Tom was watching TV, I went outdoors to tend the dog and found the back yard awash." Tom had "adjusted" a knob in the pool house. She shut off his TV program and made him wade with her to the pool house. Between them they discovered which valve to close, and the flood stopped.

She held the boy's shoulders and looked into his eyes. "I am a Two Time Teller," she said. "I tell you once and if you don't mind, I think, maybe you didn't hear me the first time, so I tell you once more. You know I said *twice* not to touch anything in the pool house. Two times telling is enough. After this, if you don't pay attention the second time, I'll pack your bag and take you to the airport to go home."

The pool house incident was midweek. At the end of the planned visit, Paula was surprised when Tom embraced her before getting on the plane. "You're my favorite grandma," he said. "The other one doesn't have any fun with me."

Fulfilling Promises

Steve's grandson, Joey, six years old, visited them during his mother's hospitalization and the first week of her being home with Joey's baby brother. Joey came into Steve's woodshop where he was finishing bookcases for the home library.

"Can you make bunk beds, too?" asked Joey.

"Just about anything that's wood, I can make," Grandfather assured him.

"Then please make bunk beds for my room. When my new brother gets big enough I want him to sleep in my room with me. Make a good ladder, too."

Grandfather promised to consult with Joey's parents. A year

later Steve and Joey's grandmother towed a U-Haul trailer loaded with Steve's custom-made bunk beds and a ladder 200 miles to Joey's home.

Joey was delighted and invited Steve to use the bottom bunk whenever he visited until little brother was old enough to sleep on it. "I get the top bunk because you're too old to climb the ladder," he explained to Steve.

The "Rules" of Tradition

"It wasn't anything we were required to do by the grandkids or their parents, but we made it a rule for ourselves and it became a tradition," says Nancy. "Mac and I were still young enough in our retirement to take long trips in our RV. Sometimes we would be gone from home as much as three or four months. We were based in Oregon. Our grandchildren were in Georgia and Utah and we couldn't see them as often as we'd like.

"Here is what we did to let the grandkids know we loved them and were always thinking of them. We told the three older ones from the time they were very young that when each reached the age of ten they could chose a special vacation. We called it the Trip-at-Ten-Vacation. We took them wherever they wanted to go. We designated age ten because by then they can follow directions such as, 'If we get separated, we will be under the big clock waiting for you.'

"The oldest chose Disneyland. Since he lived in Georgia, we flew there and took him to Disney World in Florida. After a couple of days there, we drove to Cape Canaveral to learn about the space program, and on to the Florida Everglades to see the native wildlife.

"This tradition continued with the other two older grandkids and sometimes we flew them to our home to explore the Oregon Coast, visit the redwood forests and go fishing or kayaking.

"All three are now in college. We always saved pictures of our adventures together and as each turned eighteen we created a photo album for him. The boys report that 'turning ten was the very best birthday ever.'

"Now the youngest two, both girls, are three and five. In a few years they'll have their turns and we look forward to continuing the tradition of Trip-at-Ten."

Hosting Grandkids when Home Is a Retirement Complex

Years ago when my husband and I were ready to retire we had custody of our fifteen-year-old grandson. This was to be of indefinite duration as his parents were in counseling and settling marital difficulties. We loved Mark dearly and got along well. He seemed to prefer being with us to being with either parent. We had bargained to purchase a charming home on the golf course in one of the Dell Web Retirement Communities. Fortunately, before we made the final decision, we learned that no children under eighteen could be housed for more than two weeks at that location. We changed our plans, of course, and remained in our old home with Mark living with us until he graduated from high school and enrolled in a distant college.

Many years later, after my husband died, I moved to a retirement home on the California Central Coast. I looked forward to the first visit from ten- and eight-year-old grandchildren and their mother. It took only minutes for me to show daughter and grandkids around the small, cozy apartment I had "graduated" to after years of keeping up a home and yard.

I was in "residential heaven." Here my meals were prepared and served restaurant style. No grocery shopping, no dishes to wash. I had a coffee maker and micro in my apartment in case I didn't want to go to a regular meal. I had beautiful views of distant green hills and a little patio for potted plants. Refuse was picked up at my door twice a week. I proudly showed my visiting family around and explained all the pluses to my daughter.

As she and I sat chatting, the kids played games on my computer but we paid no attention to what else they were doing until my telephone rang. It was the desk calling. "What's the emergency?" was the anxious question.

"No emergency," I said. Then I realized what had happened.

"Sorry, visiting grandkids," I added as I remembered the bank of buttons in my bathroom that were one of the amenities offered in my new home. The kids had pushed the emergency button that signaled trouble in my apartment.

I explained to the grandkids what had happened and told them the most important rule for visiting grandma: "Do not push any buttons unless I tell you to."

As I settled into living there I met many grandparents who lived at a distance from their grandchildren. Pets were allowed as permanent residents with tenants, (cats indoors, dogs on a leash) but no visitors were allowed to stay more than a month.

Among the amenities were a swimming pool, a crafts room, a laundry room, a card room, and a library. Child guests had to be supervised. Nobody under eighteen could even do the laundry for Grandmother unless Gram went along.

New friend Edith and I chatted about a recent visit from her grandchildren. They loved the elevator and gleefully rode up and down from her third-floor apartment—but she had to be with them. They enjoyed the swimming pool for hours but no lifeguard was provided. "I just lathered myself in sunscreen and sat at the edge of the pool reading. The only thing I could have done if a kid was in trouble was to throw him a life preserver from the side and scream for help. Much as I love those kids, two days was as much as I could manage in supervising their visit."

Belle, another new acquaintance, told me flat-out that she welcomed her grandkids for visits but only when their mother or father came along to manage the supervision details.

I called a couple of retirement complexes near my present home in Arizona to check out their policy about stay-over visitors. One manager could have been speaking for each of them: "When you move in here, the apartment is yours. You can have visitors of any age for as long as you want, but no live-in children or grandchildren who would go to work or school from our complex. They would not be visitors then, but residents—and ours is a retirement home."

A California retirement home I consulted has recently completely refurbished the grounds at their complex, including adding a heated spa as well as an enlarged swimming pool and power doors for the lobby. Visiting children love to test the doors and their magical auto openers, and swim in the pool. No lifeguard means visiting children must be supervised and there's a thirty-day limit for visitors to any resident's apartment.

Anxieties–Parents' and Grandparents'

A primary goal is mutual understanding between parents and grandparents. All have concerns about the health, happiness, and safety of the children in their care. Both parents and grandparents must list or verbalize their concerns and exchange information in advance of the visit. If Billy has developed a passion for striking matches, all adult parties should be forewarned. If Sally is a climber, grandpa should be there if the kid decides to climb the back yard apple tree. Honest communication meets most problems before they occur.

Chapter 3

Grandmother Ingenuity

Rewarding and productive grandparent-grandchild relationships evolve in as many different ways as there are grandparents and grandchildren.

Shared Shopping

Evelyn writes, "My oldest granddaughter attends University of Nevada near my home in Reno. She is far beyond the stage of wanting to 'hang out' with grandmother. Through the summer I saved 20 percent-off household goods coupons from the newspaper. When she gets back from school this fall, we'll use the coupons to get the stuff she needs for her dorm room. We'll have fun together with a purpose that will appeal to her. It will be a pleasant connection I will not have on a regular basis when she is in school."

City vs. Country

For a city dweller like Bea who lives in a condo overlooking the Pacific, hosting country grandson Melvin, ten, from Cottonwood, Arizona, was fraught with concern. Accustomed to walking to his friends' homes and school by himself, Melvin could not understand his grandmother's restrictions. He insisted that he could go alone to the beach, only two short blocks away. Bea accompanied him, dragging a beach chair and umbrella. However, going to the beach as often and staying as long as Melvin wanted was too much for her.

Seeking an activity in which she could sit down and still supervise the boy, she arranged for a to-and-from trip aboard the Coast Starlight passenger train north to Oceanside. Melvin had never ridden a train. She also took him to the San Diego Wild Animal Park. The boy was fascinated with the tram and the animals. As Bea says, "Riding the train and the tram through the animal park, sitting in a comfortable seat, was much easier for me than trekking down to the sand every morning."

The shore remained the boy's favorite place. Sandwiching beach visits between other adventures where Bea could be comfortable saved the vacation. She also took him to Sea World where they could sit in the bleachers and watch the dolphins perform.

Country vs. City

For my granddaughter Emily, who lived in Los Angeles, visiting us at our small dairy ranch in California was the best vacation in the world. Her mother, our daughter, had regaled her with the fun she'd had in 4-H when she raised a calf on our little ranch. When Emily was twelve, she came to visit us as soon as school was out. Supervising her exploration of the ranch and answering her many questions was so time-consuming, we grandparents couldn't get our chores done.

We had a neighbor Beverly, about the same age as Emily. I invited her for cake and ice cream so the two could get acquainted. Beverly's questions and interests centered on what Emily did for fun in the city. Emily didn't want to talk about movies and riding the famous Angels Flight railway. She wanted to know about the goats and pigs in Beverly's backyard pens. Beverly reluctantly took Emily to see these animals but later let me know that Emily was 'boring.'

Finally, I worked out a plan that kept Emily happily engaged.

Ours was an old fashioned business. We still delivered milk door-to-door to some customers.

Emily's grandfather and I took turns with deliveries. We asked Emily to be our delivery girl. We showed her which customers wanted the milk placed on the back step and which ones wanted it taken inside to the refrigerator. She was enchanted with her new job. We gave her a small salary for her help, which was truly a great help for us. She came back the following summer for her "summer job" on the ranch.

Providing Emily with a job that was a real contribution to the family's workload was rewarding for all.

Last Minute Accommodation

On the day that Maria (Queen Mum of her local branch of the Red Hat Society) was to host the luncheon for her group, her grandson arrived a day early for a week's stay. Maria had no time to find another sitter for eight-year-old Bobby, so she initiated a plan with the boy's cooperation. He would "help grandma" by wearing a red baseball cap and a purple T-shirt. He was to greet the ladies at the door of the restaurant as they arrived in their red hats and purple outfits. He would guide them to the section of the restaurant where they were to gather.

"He rose to the challenge, beautifully," says Maria. "I was amazed at how well he handled this bit of play-acting. He stood outside the restaurant door and to each arrival, said 'Welcome to the Curvaceous Cuties Red Hat Luncheon. I'll show you where you are meeting.' Of course, he charmed the lot and sat beside me as I presided at the meeting and the luncheon."

As with giving Emily a job on the ranch, giving Bobby a special job offered a learning experience for him and a delight for the Red Hat ladies.

Sitter Service Grandparenting

"My husband and I had a standing arrangement to take care of our two grandchildren while their parents, our son and his wife, went boating and water skiing on Lake Powell," Marcella reports. When the boys were five and three, the beloved blanket of the younger was accidentally left in the parents' car. Tears flowed and sobs shook the little shoulders.

"I had an inspiration. 'I wonder what your blanket feels as it rides away without you?' I asked. The idea was just different enough to halt the sobs. 'Maybe we could write a story about it. What would we call it?'

"'The Lost Blanket,' piped up the older boy.

"All agreed and we postponed tooth-brushing and bedtime to gather around my computer screen for a creative-writing session. We hit a snag when the older boy suggested the blanket got caught on the spines of a cactus.

"'Nooo,' howled little brother. 'No hurts, no troubles for my blanket.'

"A seriously delayed bedtime saw the adventures of the blanket written, copied and resting beside the pillows of two proud authors—three, if you count the grandma who hit on the solution to a sticky problem."

Sitting a Rambunctious Grandchild

Ann got into trouble with her son and daughter-in-law. She had agreed to care for her three-year-old grandson one weekend while his mother and father visited a nearby resort. "He is adorable," says Ann, "but he was into everything, opening cupboard doors, and switching lights on and off. He loved to climb the stairway, lean over the balcony and shout, 'Catch me, Grandma.'

"At seventy years of age, I just wasn't up to the chase," says Ann. She finally invented an activity that delighted the child and gave her rest. She took him to her car in the driveway, held him on her lap and let him pretend to drive. This included putting the key into the ignition, moving the gear shift and turning the wheel. It became the child's first request from then on.

Her son and daughter-in-law complained that after this session the child screamed at being put into his car seat. He wanted to sit in mommy's or daddy's lap and "drive the car."

"This operation gave me much needed rest," says Ann. "The car wasn't moving, of course, but I can see how this adventure might lead to unwanted consequences."

To Host or Not to Host

Speaking of "rambunctious," not all grandparents–long or short distance–are created equal. Sandra reports that she and her husband happily visited their daughter, husband, and grandchildren 500 miles away, but had to refuse the daughter's request to leave the youngest boy with them so the parents and the two older children could take a trip together. "The child was great in his own home," Sandra says, "but we simply could not keep up with him in ours. I feared for his life when he wanted to slide down our banister and climb the back fence. Our excuses ranged from prior commitments, to Grandpa's diabetes, to my club work. I'm sure daughter Kathy saw through this and stopped asking. When the boy was seven, we accepted a visit. He and his grandfather went fishing together. He behaved well and they had fun together."

Thanklessness

Leslie, a widow, lives 1,000 miles from her Idaho grandchildren. "I really don't think I'm a very successful example of long-distance grandparenting," she says. "I send gifts and money but seldom get a thank you for anything. I must have failed somewhere. I've even put little notes in with the money asking them to tell me what they buy. Perhaps it's a generational thing. I always taught their mother and my son to send thank you notes and stood over them until they did so.

"In discussions with my friends, we all agree that it's easier to give money because we have no idea what they have or the sizes they wear or what their tastes are. I've tried phone calls but it's very hard to catch children or parents at home these days. Leaving messages that are never returned tends to make one feel sort of left out of the circle."

Re-evaluating Gifts

Thea writes, "There was a time that my eldest son's family had no money and we spent hundreds of dollars on them to make sure they had a good Christmas. For several years, we bought items for their home, and major toys like tricycles for the children. In the last fifteen years of their marriage, six babies later, we've only received one thank-you note. Both of us are burned out by their lack of gratitude. We're re-evaluating our gift giving.

"In fact, we are re-evaluating many things in relationship to our grown children. They seem to have preconceived ideas about how we are to conduct our lives. Only two of the five are completely supportive of us. We feel we are certainly due recognition for having survived rearing them and giving them the gift of life.

"I've lived long enough to know that these bumps in relationships will pass, but they have left their mark on grandpa and me. It actually makes it easier to be a long distance from them. Quite frankly, I can't fathom how we could live in the same town with any of them. I'll just keep working to cement relationships with the grandchildren as they mature."

"Queen of Nature" Grandmother

Grandmother Dena records a different story about gifts for grandkids. "I do not feel I'm called upon to present gifts each time I visit," she says. "For birthdays and Christmas, I always ask the parents what the children might like rather than try to guess. It is fascinating how wide-ranged the grandkids' interests are. I love to give magazine subscriptions or books. The magazines give them six to a dozen gifts in one. The books I've ordered so far this year include one about a famous physicist, one on surfers' code of conduct, an animal encyclopedia. I have also given a subscription to *National Geographic*.

"I'm very *'simpatico'* with one grandson in rural Oklahoma," she continues. "He is fascinated with bugs, as I am. So it was a natural for me to send him a good butterfly net and a guide book on butterflies in his state for his ninth birthday—along with the information that a butterfly is not a 'bug' but a Lepidoptera. I received a thank-you note from him addressed to 'Grandma, The Queen of Nature. I can't wait until I use the net and all the information the book gave me. Love, Robert.'"

Borders, No Barrier

Widow Marge lives 100 miles north of the U.S.-Mexico border. Her son and his wife and three grandchildren live in Baja California, about 50 miles south of the border.

"I invited them to my home for dinner last Sunday," says Marge. "The family responded that they wanted to take me out to dinner because it was Grandparents' Day. That was news to me. I told them that I already had dinner ready and they could take me out another time. They came and we spent seven happy hours together. My sixteen-year-old grandson salvaged some computer files that I thought I had permanently lost. After dinner we played dominos and had late snacks. It was lovely.

"Next week, when my son is at work, his wife and the three children, ranging in age from sixteen to nineteen, and I will go to the official office near the border to get my Port Pass. It will be good for two years, making it easy to go back and forth across the border. This Port Pass is a part of our government's Homeland Security system. It verifies that I am who I say I am and live where I say I do, and that I have enough money to meet my needs—even though I am a U.S. citizen. If I didn't have the pass and tried to return to the U.S. from Mexico, I'd have to wait in a line up to four hours. With my Port Pass, I'll wait no more than twenty minutes each way. The pass is not free, but it does save a lot of time and hassle. I am closer to these grandchildren as they near adulthood than when they were little."

Four Hours to Togetherness

Courtney works hard to stay in touch with her grandchildren, three boys, ages six, ten, and twelve. They live about four hours away. They don't yet come alone to visit so are always brought by one or both parents. "We travel to them more often than the other way around," says Courtney, "primarily because we have the time while both parents are fully employed. We usually manage to visit once a month.

"A big concern is being able to influence their lives from a distance. To provide quality time, we have initiated outings with each child individually. Last August we took Timmy, the six-year-old to San Diego for five days. We did kid-friendly activities—Sea World, the zoo, the Wild Animal Park. His mom, our daughter, came along. Her husband and the two older boys went to Europe to visit the other grandparents. Our visit with Timmy was kind of a consolation prize because he didn't get to fly with his dad and brothers.

"In July we took the ten-year-old to a mountain lake for four days to do whatever he wanted. This turned out to be four days of fishing.

"When visiting them at either home, we try to plan activities that involve the whole family. Our last time there, we went to a nearby park and played softball, mixed teams, adults and kids. All had fun. The six-year-old held his own with the adults. He even pitched.

"The grandkids seem always glad to see us. We feel it is important to show how much we care—not only with visits—but also with cards, phone calls, e-mails and photos. Additional concerns," says Courtney, "are financial challenges their parents face. We try to add extras, such as savings accounts for the grandkids to help them learn the value of saving—such as earning interest, little as it is these days."

✓ Hostess with the Mostest

Grandmother Bonnie plans an annual summer visit to her three grandchildren, ages six, eight, and nine, and their parents who live three states away in Kansas. She began this plan when the oldest was seven. She reserves a room at a motel in their town. The motel has a swimming pool, outdoor shuffleboard, and card room with a pool table. There, she hosts the grandchildren—one at a time—for three days each.

"When granddaughter Amy is with me, we spend most of our time in the swimming pool, her favorite, as the family does not have a pool," Bonnie says. "We also shop for a pretty new bathing suit before her visit begins.

"The two older children are boys. They are good swimmers and don't need as much supervision as Amy. I'm teaching the older boy to play pool, but the younger one isn't tall enough and I don't want to be liable for cue holes in the pool table cover, so he and I play shuffleboard and dominos in the club room."

For meals, they go out to restaurants. "Each kid feels he's had a real vacation even though we're on the outskirts of the town where they live," Bonnie adds. "If there are any problems, we're near enough that I can contact their parents."

Dining Togetherness

When I last visited my children and grandchildren in Washington state, I took the entire family to dinner as a small "thanks" for housing and feeding me during my stay with them.

Grandson Miles, a college freshman, asked if he could bring his girlfriend to our dinner. Of course, I agreed. Seven of us—two sons and wives, grandson Miles' and his friend Martha—gathered happily around a large table on the restaurant's quiet vine-hung patio. Afterward, in thanking me, Martha confided that her family never sat down for a meal together. Her mother keeps the refrigerator stocked with frozen dinners, vegetables, fruits, "and lots of pizza. We all just help ourselves whenever we're hungry."

This was new to me, but my daughter-in-law explained, "This is the TV generation, Mom. Bob and I have insisted that Miles and his older brother obey our rules: The TV goes off at dinner time and no TV or cell phones are allowed in the dining room. I know that their friends' families rarely have a meal together—except maybe Thanksgiving and Christmas."

"Maybe sharing around the table is no longer desirable," I said. I didn't admit it, but now, living alone, I often eat my meals in front of the TV.

"We're probably a vanishing breed," she added with a shrug and a smile.

This is what we mean when we advise "different strokes." Circumstances create different answers for long- or short-distance grandparents, their children, and their grandkids.

Nana's Treasure Box

Veronica reports a different way of dealing with a dinner-hour problem. "When granddaughter Liz turned eight, her mother brought her by plane to visit us in Idaho. We were to drive her back to Michigan after a month's vacation with us. She is a precocious child and quite spoiled, it seemed to me. For the few meals her mother ate with us, the child would take one bite of food, leave the table on some pretext or another, sometimes to get her doll, to go to the bathroom, or just to go to the window and look out. Her mother paid no attention to this behavior, but it bothered me. Her father, our son, had always stayed at the dinner table until he was excused. Liz' mother is a lovely woman but one who apparently has not been reared with any such dinner protocols. As soon as the child's mother left, I came up with a plan. I placed a shoe-box covered in bright paper on the table, like a centerpiece.

"'What's that?' Liz asked as soon as we sat down to eat.

"As soon as we serve our plates, I will tell you.

"I put meat and vegetables on her plate in small amounts, asking each time which ones she liked best. 'More potatoes,' she said when I gave her one piece. I complied. As soon as her plate was satisfactorily covered with food, she jumped up from the table.

"I asked her to come back and sit down if she wanted to know what was in Nana's treasure box. At first it was just a box in the middle of the table, but as soon as I said 'treasure box' she sat down at her place.

"'When you have eaten your dinner, you get to close your eyes and reach inside the box and take out one item. Everything in the box is a small, wrapped treasure just for you, but until we finish dinner and unless you stay at the table, you do not get to pick a treasure.'

"We made sure our dinner conversation involved her. We told her about the different things we could take her to see and asked if she'd like to travel on the miniature train in a small park nearby or go for a boat ride on the lake. These questions brought conversation about whether she had a miniature train ride or a lake near her home. Soon she was babbling on and on about her school and her friends—and remaining at the table as she ate. She didn't clean her plate, but she stayed in her chair—which was the object of the treasure box."

Is My Best Good Enough?

Nedra has high standards. "If I could twitch my nose like Elizabeth Montgomery in the TV program 'Bewitched' to become the perfect grandmother, I'd be a combination of many people: adventurous like Auntie Mame; beautiful like Jackie O; crafty like Martha Stewart, and warm and nurturing like my own grandmother, whose devotion made me feel as though I was her favorite.

"I'd love to be able to offer a glowing report about how terrific I am as a grandmother, how much the ten long-distance grandchildren crave my company and adore me for my wisdom, and how much fun I always am. But that would not be exactly true. It would set other grandmothers up for guilt trips and longing. All I know is that I'm doing my best. I did my best as a mother and often feel the gripping of guilt that it wasn't good enough, that I made too many mistakes, that I was too lenient or too strict. Yet, four of the five have college degrees—in computers, architecture, and the law. All are highly intelligent. The grandchildren are equally bright. They are budding musicians, straight-A students, compulsive readers and writers, and active in sports. The babies have yet to emerge, but one two-year-old shows the makings of a gymnast.

"So what do I do in my role as a long distance grandmother?

For birthdays, instead of sending gifts, I send a birthday card with two dollars for every year of age. I don't know how long this will continue before I have to set a limit, but for now it works quite well. I make sure to send one-dollar bills so it seems like a lot of money to the little ones. At Christmas, we have sent gifts in the past but I'm leaning toward sending a card for all with money so they can buy or save toward something they want."

Creating a Pillow Tradition

Moms are often too busy to teach their children to sew or cook, but these activities can create bonding experiences for grandmothers and grandkids. Most grandmothers love to share their secrets, and usually have more time and patience than the working mom or the one trying to get the family fed so she can get off to a meeting.

Grandmother Natalie has hosted granddaughters Cindy and Michelle since they were five and seven years old. They travel by plane to her North Carolina home.

Tucking the girls in their first night away from home, she sensed a touch of homesickness when Cindy asked, "Will Mommy call tomorrow?"

"That launched a tradition the girls still talk about," says Natalie. "It is important to be creative *with* the grandchildren—not just *for* them.

"'Tomorrow,' I told them, 'we will go to the store and pick out a soft pillow for each of you, then to the fabric store to choose the material to make your very own pillowcases—with special secret pockets.'

"This intrigued them enough so that, along with the story I read and their own teddy bears cuddled beside them, both went to sleep. The next day we bought pillows, then went to the fabric shop. It took at least an hour for each girl to settle on a pattern for her yard of percale. Back home, they stood beside me and watched, fascinated, as I turned on the electric sewing machine and quickly stitched up a case for each pillow. Then I introduced the idea of a secret pocket. It was for the money the Tooth Fairy would leave if she were expected to visit that year at our home or at the girls' home. Each chose where I was to place the pocket on the hem. These pillows were exclusively the property of each girl and were kept here in our home in a dresser drawer. No one else ever used their pillows. Every year we went to the fabric store for new pillow slip material, and each night they spent with us, they put their heads on their very own pillows.

"The pillow slips always have their owner's name and the year it was made machine-embroidered on the hem. At the end of their stays, I tuck the pillow slips into their suitcases and their mother put sthem away in the girls' memory chests. Now young college students, they still come to visit and still sleep on their special pillows.

"Grandparenting, whether near or far, is building memories. My own grandmother taught me so much, but mainly how to enjoy the simple things like looking down into a well and yelling to hear the echo, drawing a bucket up and enjoying the taste of that cool, clear water. I'll treasure my memories forever and I hope my granddaughters pass along the tradition of the 'pillow case parade' to their grandchildren."

Crochet Hooks and Knitting Needles

"My children's paternal grandmother made a quilt for each of my five children," Theresa recalls. "My grown children have saved and treasured these. Their grandmother had more time than I've ever had, but seeing how much these grandmother-crafted gifts mean to my kids, I am in process of crocheting an afghan for each of the eight grandkids. Two are completed for the older ones. My dream is that they will take care of them, perhaps even take them to college and on into their future homes. I have crocheted scarves for those in the cold country and just finished fulfilling a request for specific colors in a scarf.

"I adore the babies, laugh and play with the toddlers, when the families bring them or when I visit. But I am truly beginning to enjoy the intelligence of the older grandchildren. Their personalities and talents are emerging. When we were together for a recent holiday celebration, the oldest asked me to help her write a sonnet for English class. The next couldn't wait to read me her magical story. I was in 'Grandmother Heaven.'

"In every family there are bumps in the road, and balancing

acts to be performed. It hasn't been easy establishing a delicate balance between letting them know we are supportive, offering tentative suggestions for solving problems, and allowing them to make their own decisions—and face the consequences of their choices.

"The older I get, the more I realize how much I don't know, and when it comes to being a good grandparent, I just don't have the answers," says Theresa. "I do know that in family relations, 'One size does *not* fit all.' Personalities are too varied. The dynamics and organization of the family are combined in a 'people growing machine.' We get to love, forgive, repent, be humbled, supported, cherished, proud—and sometimes—rejected."

Fun in the Kitchen

Grandmother Lettie offers instructions taught early and still treasured by her grown grandchildren. A series of "lazy recipes" encouraged the grandchildren to make something that didn't require reading a grown-up cook book. "Once taught," says Lettie, "our Lazy-Angel Cake had a life of its own and its 'progeny' continues to be a hit, constantly embellished in the grandchildren's own homes."

Lazy-Angel Cake

Buy a ready-made white angel food cake. Remove it from the container by gently pressing the sides all around, lifting the entire cake out in one piece. On a large plate or cutting board, hold the cake on its side and use a serrated knife to gently slice across the cake, through the center hole, to create three or more layers.

Place the bottom layer on a serving plate, spread it with about a third of an 8-oz can of crushed pineapple and several tablespoons of Cool Whip. Top it with another layer and spread with pineapple and Cool Whip. Repeat with the third layer. Spread Cool Whip down the sides. The cake is fat-free and low in calories.

"The girls covered their cakes with store-bought sprinkles, co-

conut, or chocolate crumbles—each one decorated with artistry and enthusiasm."

Emergencies Must Be Met

Grace's son Bob, the father of her two grandchildren, phoned her in panic one day. His wife Molly, was hospitalized with a yet-undiagnosed illness. "Can you come for a few days and help me get the boys fed and off to school?" he asked.

Grace's husband, her son's stepfather, agreed that she should travel the 300 miles to be with the family. She prepared meals, read to the boys, packed their school lunches and did the laundry while Bob drove a triangle route daily from home, to Molly in the hospital, and his job as manager of an auto parts store. Molly was finally diagnosed with pneumonia but had to remain hospitalized for more than two weeks.

Molly's parents flew to California from their Montana home to take over the second week so that Grace could get back to her husband. She returned again to help when Molly came home from the hospital.

This wasn't a vacation for anybody, but it was a loving part of the long-distance grandparenting agenda. Both sets of grandparents were willing and able to help. All returned for vacation visits when Molly was thriving again.

Tool-Handy Grandma

When Constance's two grandsons come to visit each summer, she keeps them out of the kitchen except for meals. An amateur tool-master, she is on call in her neighborhood for carpentry repairs, lock installations, and fence-mending. ("Real fences," she says, "not psychological ones.") She built a tool shed on the side of her garage, poured the concrete floor, and erected studding and siding. "I love working outdoors, the feel of wood, and tools in my hands," she says.

Last summer the visiting grandsons, Grant, fourteen, and Toby, twelve, went with her to the local Build & Save for materials to build and hang a gate that opens into her back yard vegetable garden. They also built an arched latticework to go over the gateway. Under her guidance they used an electric drill, a saw, screws, screw drivers, hammers and nails.

"They learned something about precision in measuring, and how to use a square to line the holes up right.

"When they come next summer," Constance says, "the rambler rose will be up on the lattice they built and I think by then I'll be ready to build a gazebo beside the garden. My son and his wife, the kids' parents, know about and approve of my putting the kids to work. My son's job involves lots of travel so he does not have time to teach the boys about using tools. We're not violating any child labor laws. Each year the kids call to ask, 'What are we building this summer, Gram?' They love it and they are learning real skills they'll never get in school these days. If they still want to come for visits when they're older and if they get really good at tool use, they may be able to earn money right here in my neighborhood or in their own. It's amazing how much extra change you can pick up being tool-handy."

Easter Basket Tradition

For many years, Velma lived within a few miles of her three children. Then health problems forced her to move to a coastal suburb more than 300 miles away. Her old home had been site of an annual Easter egg hunt. She continued this tradition on the coast. Now the families gather the day before Easter and the kitchen is dedicated to boiling and dying eggs. The older grandchildren mix the dyes, trace names on the colored eggs and dip them. The eggs are placed in a huge basket in the middle of the dining room table. Some time in the night, the Easter Bunny hides the eggs along with little gifts in the adjacent oak grove. The children take their baskets and search. The one who stumbles on a gift without his name has to keep the secret and keep searching. Meanwhile Grandmother Velma and her daughters prepare Easter breakfast. The hunt over, children and adults gather at the table. Each opens his gift and announces his total of eggs.

"I'm so pleased they still want to do this," says Velma. "Of course the teens no longer believe in the Easter Bunny, but they are pledged not to destroy the story for the two little ones. The Easter weekend has become such a family tradition, we'll probably keep it even when the kids are too old for the hunt."

✓ Picture This!

"My latest projects," reports Grandmother Rose, "are hand-crafted books. The grandkids visit us one at a time, a girl, eight, and a boy, twelve, in the summer. As soon as each leaves, I start compiling a book with pictures that document the visit. I create a story line with a few words of text and a large photo on each page. These preserve memories of what we did together—the hikes, visits to the mall and the wild animal park. Even though the locations are pretty much the same for each child, the pictures and experiences are different for each. The books are presented as gifts at the next Christmas.

"After four years, each child has a small library of memories, and one of the highlights of family gatherings at Christmas is reviewing past years' albums along with receiving a new one," Rose says.

Annual Hayride Brings Them Back

The ideas that put lovely bows of memory on the ties that bind are as numerous and inventive as the individuals who conceive them. Grandma Reba responded to our request for information about what she did with her grandchildren with, "Oh nothing special." However, when we cited a few of the responses already received, she told of taking the grandkids on a hayride. She and Grandpa Clem live in a rural community that holds an annual fair. Among the highlights is a hay wagon trip to an orchard where the riders can harvest their own apples from trees especially set aside for the adventure. "That has become a tradition when the grandkids come and the oldest ones, now in their teens, still look forward to a hayride."

Chapter 4

Risks and Rewards of Grandparent Advice

First, a Few Rewards

I was about twelve when my maternal grandmother, Esther, came for her regular two-month visit. She always treated me like an adult, even though I often did not comprehend the adult concepts that she shared.

My most unforgettable exchange with her was a truth that has been an inspiration all of my life. We were sitting on the front porch watching the sun set over the mountains on the west side of the narrow valley in which we lived. Clouds had gathered on the tops of the opposite range. They were pink and lavender, and changed shapes as we watched. Grandmother gestured toward the clouds. "See how beautiful they are?" she said.

"Yes, Grandma, they are beautiful. One looks like a pink zeppelin," I replied.

She turned to me and, in solemn tones, said, "Enjoy seeing them and remember them, because no matter how many times you see beautiful clouds, you will never again in your lifetime see them in exactly the same shape and size and color as you see them now."

She took my hand and, looking deep into my eyes said, "And that is like you. You are the only one in the world exactly like you and the only one who will ever be exactly like you."

This was profound to me then, and remains so today. It inspired me more than anything else in my childhood years to do the best I could with whatever native gifts I had and to pick up the pieces and go on whenever I fell flat on my face.

School Assignment Assistance

Peggy, who lives in Kansas, cites a situation in which her Seattle grandson asked for advice before she even thought to offer it. "Alex was blessed with an English teacher whose assignment to her seventh grade class was that each student was to find a writing partner. I was delighted when Alex chose me. He first phoned to explain. There would be four letters, each on a particular topic. I, as the partner, would have to share my experiences and feelings on the same topic.

"His first letter was quite formal. The topic was to share his goals, dreams, and aspirations. The letter was painfully honest and his goals gripped my heart. He talked about career choices and qualities he wanted to have as a man. In my response, I told him that at his age, I didn't even think of goals, dreams, and aspirations. I explained how life was in the late 1940s, how different things were then, in education and other ways. There was no talk of college for me, because I knew I had to get a job and help my parents financially.

"His second letter was about future problems he might have. He really shared from his heart. I replied that at his age, I felt awkward. I hated the way I looked, and I had trouble making friends. I told him what I learned from each problem that I faced.

"His next letter was about a personal challenge or challenges that changed the way he viewed himself or the world around him. His last letter had to describe the most important life lesson he had learned so far and to ask me for my most important advice. He asked also if we could continue writing after this project was over. 'Of course!' I replied. He shared so openly, I almost wept.

"He asked my most important advice. I told him that I would not tell him to be a good person because I knew he already was good. He loved and respected his parents and had shown that he had developed a good work ethic. Rather, I told him to expect transitions in life, to expect change—the only constant in life. We all cope with transitions and we must be flexible. Change is not the end of the world. It is often the beginning of wonderful new things—another job, starting a business, finding a new career and new friends.

"This letter exchange with Alex across the miles was a wonderful experience for me and, apparently, also for him. We still correspond, but his life is getting busier so letters are few. He is accepting and progressing happily with this 'change' between the two of us."

Risking Advice

From Joann comes this report. "My son and daughter-in-law, both with Ivy League graduate degrees, live 300 miles from us. When they produced a darling baby, I flew to visit every few months. More and more I realized that this baby was a 'project' their academic skills had not prepared them for—infant rashes and a sucking problem that kept him from gaining weight. I watched them struggle, keeping my body language and certainly my tongue from making the situation worse. But when I heard my brilliant son apply his skill at sarcasm to his beloved eighteen-month-old, I decided I must protest.

"Son, I know you love this baby, but I'm not sure you like him," I said.

"'Well, if you're going to talk like that, we'd better get his mother in on the conversation.'

"I gulped and chose my words carefully. They listened courteously and did what any self-respecting academic parents would do—searched the Internet and found a series of child-rearing classes. These were a great success, putting son and daughter-in-law in touch with a wise instructor and other couples like themselves, who shared their frustrations and successes. The child is twelve now, has a younger brother, and is a delight. I'm full of admiration for these young parents who faced a difficult, emotion-laden situation head-on and didn't hold resentment toward me when, however awkwardly, I intervened."

Advice from Their Grandkids' Parents

"My husband and I live 800 miles from two sons, daughters-in-law, and four grandsons," says Evelyn. It was our dream to build a cabin halfway between them in Denver and our home in California, a place for building memories over the years. We bought a half-acre lot on a trout stream, and spent happy hours sketching house plans. Unfortunately, the dream was slated for early demise.

"One son's words were: 'We can't get away that often, Mom. Not enough vacation time from our jobs, summer sports, and other activities for the kids. Our own dream is to hike in the Rockies or the High Sierra every year when the boys are old enough.'

"We got it. We grandparents are the mobile, less-scheduled side of this situation. With a sad look back, we sold the lot in favor of visiting the two Colorado families two or three times a year and welcoming them to our home every August. This summer, after one family's trek over Army Pass south of Mount Whitney, including the two boys, they drove the extra miles to spend a few days with us. I hugged our son saying, 'Thanks for taking the side trip here. I know you drove seven extra hours to get to us.'

"'What do you mean, Grandma, a side trip?' said the eight-year-old. 'Coming to see you and Grandpa is the main thing—for me, anyway.'

"I think he'd 'had it' with backpacking and I guess we'll keep this arrangement."

Advice by Example

Brenna's husband Glen, is not the blood grandfather of her six-teen-year-old grandson, Bill but, according to Brenna, he is "my port in a storm" when it comes to deciding what to do next about the boy.

Brenna says, "Bill spent last Christmas in a therapeutic boarding school for 'soft' drug abuse and assorted hell-raising. He managed to avoid the juvenile justice system, but barely. Last summer, after spending two weeks with us in the Pacific Northwest, we put him on the train for home to Los Angeles. But he never arrived. Instead, he ran away with some friends to Korea Town, where he was beaten and robbed of his cell phone. When he was found two weeks later, his parents intervened and sent him to Outward Bound in Utah. Then, in time for the holidays he was moved to a boarding school in Saint George. I prayed there was something I could do, by just visiting him.

"Glen and I got up early the day after Christmas. In driving rain, we got to Saint George by early evening. I was appalled when I saw the place. It was a strip mall. They wouldn't let us see Bill that evening but allowed us a three-hour pass the next day after school.

"Bill's first reaction was, 'You came all this way for me?' which says a lot about his self esteem. We saw him twice in the three days we were there and went hiking and talked a lot, went out for crab and pizza and played cards in Pizza Hut, as he was not allowed to go to our hotel or the movies.

"When we left, Bill hugged Glen and me like he didn't want to let go.

"You live with uncertainty when there's a kid on drugs in your life, but so far the story seems to have a hopeful ending. Bill came home from Utah in February and finished out the school year. He took two classes in summer school and aced both of them. He's always liked to cook and while at the boarding school, he received instruction from the cook there. Bill now works as a cook's helper at a rest home after school and on weekends."

Advice through Support

Like Brenna, Grandmother Mary has a grandson Bruce, who is in trouble. "Bruce's father was killed in an auto accident when the boy was six," says Mary. "This may be a factor since his mother remarried. Her new husband is great and good to the two grandsons, but Bruce, seventeen, is in juvenile detention.

"He is super smart," she adds. "From the time he was a pre-teen, I enjoyed having him visit. We had great talks about religion and philosophy. He was always bored with school. He was smarter than his classmates and smarter, I think, than some of his teachers. I never would have suspected that he had the desire or the nerve that it must take to rob a bank. But that's what he tried to do. It's probably good that he was caught."

Mary, a professional writer, has never handed out admonitions or advice but she has now taken on the loving chore of writing daily to Bruce. "My letter is the first thing I do, before breakfast, every morning. I hope that knowing how much his grandfather and I care for him and his future will help him get through this difficult time."

Mixed Marriage Responsibilities

Jean and Jerry have two grown sons and two grown daughters. One son, George, who lives 400 miles away, is married to Kippy, of Chinese descent.

"Their biracial children live within two miles of Kippy's parents and have always seen them more often and been closer to them than to us." says Jean. "We have totally supported this affiliation. After all, we can't duplicate that closeness. The older of the two grandsons, George, Jr., came to visit us when he was fourteen.

"Even though we live within ten miles of the Pacific, Jerry took him fishing at a mountain stream, feeling that the trek along a stream bank would be more interesting than sitting at the end of a pier. The boy caught a trout and Jerry added it to his catch. George enjoyed the fish dinner and thanked us for the visit, but he was not enthusiastic enough about us or fishing to ask for a return visit. Now an adult, he is employed in the same town where we live. We see him often. He recollects warmly that single fishing trip, and he and Jerry have scheduled a several-days campout in the mountains for next summer."

When Grandmothers Clash

"At times," says Grandmother Kate, "I'd like to wring the neck of my daughter-in-law's mother. She and I both live within walking distance of my son and her daughter and our four grandchildren.

"I hate to admit it, but we have clashed over who is the 'best, most-loved' grandmother. We are both widowed and lonely and should be friends in support of our children and especially the grandchildren. If I give one granddaughter a doll, the other grandma gives her a bigger, more expensive one on her next birthday. She criticizes the colors I choose for one grandchild or another, not to me, but I hear about it. The other day little Marie told me, 'Grandma Polly (the other grandma) said this color doesn't look good on me.'

"I know this puts our kids, the parents, in a bind," Kate continues. "They keep count of how many times they ask me to sit the grandkids, how many times they ask Polly. I doubt that she can be persuaded, but I, for one, am going to seek professional counseling. We must not let our clashes get in the way of the happiness of our son and daughter and the rewarding development of the grandchildren."

Every situation is different and sometimes any grandparent advice offered is rebuffed so strongly that total estrangement results. Each of us must consider the pros and cons and what can be gained for all parties. If significant gain is not probable, it may be best for grandparents to let the situation ride and take themselves off on a cruise or an adventure. Time may be the straw that is eventually woven into gold.

Chapter 5

New Parents, New Grandparents, and New Mix of Kids

In today's society, widowed or divorced parents often remarry, inheriting the new partner's children and creating multiple sets of grandparents. New relationships are developed on all sides of an extended family.

Where Do Grandparents Fit in a Split Between Parents?

"It got complicated for us," says Gloria. "I was very close to my daughter's two children when we lived near them in Rhode Island. Even when we moved west, I wrote regularly to them, reminding them of our trips to the shore we had taken near their home, and telling them of similar trips Gramps and I make here on the West Coast. When the little girls were five and eight, our daughter divorced their father. A year later, she announced her plan to marry a man with two young sons.

"My husband and I attended the wedding, but the time was too short for us to become acquainted with the two new grandsons. When I introduced myself as his new grandma, eight-year-old Grant said, 'I already have two grandmas and two grandpas. Do I need more?'"

Gloria adds, "I don't want to slight the new grandchildren but I do not know them and I can't write long letters of the kind I once sent to the granddaughters."

She has adopted one solution to the problem of new grandkids living far away. She sends frequent short notes to all four children about the grandparent adventures. And she keeps a "letter diary" in which she dates the adventures she and their grandfather are having. She puts them into scrapbooks for when the girls are older. Her daughter says that the boys are close to their mother's parents and all seem happy with the arrangement.

"I guess everybody is satisfied that there are enough grandparents to go around," concludes Gloria.

When the Split Takes the Grandchild Far Away

Paul and Faye are *long*, long-distance grandparents. Their half-Japanese granddaughter lives in Japan with her mother. Their son, the father of the little girl, and his Tokyo-employed wife are separated. The mother speaks fluent English and the child is learning the language slowly. Paul and Faye e-mail weekly with the mother, relaying information about their lives in Texas, inquiring about her life and welfare there. The child's mother translates for the four-year-old and replies for both of them. She frequently sends digital photos.

Mother, child, and grandparents plan a reunion next summer in Hawaii to celebrate little Kayli's fifth birthday and get reacquainted with mother and child, whom they have not seen for two years.

"Kayli is not any less our granddaughter just because she lives so far away and because her parents chose to live apart. We stay away from discussing the parents' relationship," Paul adds.

When Grandma Is the Go-Between

Gail, a teacher, offers this advice. "Supporting a grandchild who is the rope in a tug-of-war between parents isn't that difficult if one follows a single, basic rule: *Nobody is the bad guy.*

"Two of my grandchildren are 400 miles away. Their parents are going through a stressful time in their lives. The girls' time with me is like recess from school, where they escape their parents' strife and simply have a good time, shopping, going to the movies, the park, the mountains, and the beach.

"When my grandkids bring up something such as, 'I was supposed to get my nails done with Mama, but my new Daddy wouldn't let me,' it isn't necessary to make a judgment. The kids may be testing to see where my loyalties lie. Never give this away. Just listen and redirect the conversation.

"'If you had your nails done, what color would you pick? Really? I like pink too. Let's look for a pink shirt for you when we go shopping.'

"Most important: Hug! Compliment! Hug! Compliment! Hug! Encourage! Hug!

"I've been on both sides—the frazzled, exhausted, wounded parent who becomes, for a time, emotionally unavailable to her children, and the strong, supportive grandmother who has lots of love to shower on innocent children. Grandparents are in the unique position to be close—offering lots of love—but distant *if they are wise*—in verbalized judgment. This means nonverbal communication as well. No fair shaking your head or rolling your eyes."

Margaret found herself in a similar situation. "I made myself stay objective when my daughter split with her husband. This was partly for selfish reasons. I did not want to find myself shut out of visitation with my eight-year-old grandson. I had to take on the strange but somehow sensible role of physical mediator in all those awful, stressful, ugly visits to the courthouse when daughter and soon-to-be-ex son-in-law sat at opposite ends of the hallway. I was the one who walked young Seth, back and forth between the two parents. I never shut down lines of communication with my son-in-law, never told him what a jerk I thought he was, although I was sorely tempted. I just kept things agreeable and casual.

"All the parties, including the judge, agreed that Seth should stay with me as I was the only person able to demonstrate neutrality when the boy's mom and dad needed mandatory time-out to take parenting classes. I had to interact with both sides objectively and I made it work for Seth's sake. I feel that we grandparents should always do what's right for the sake of the children."

Standing By

"Our son's divorce isn't final," Angela reports, "but he's moved out and has his daughter Janie half the time. They now live near us and come to dinner once a week. Janie is having a tough time because her mother is being incredibly mean and taking a lot of her anger out on the daughter. We're trying to be supportive and keep out mouths shut. It's difficult but that's what all grandparents should do."

Plan for the Long Term

Ellen and Marty Moore have two grandsons whose troubled mother left home for a number of months, just as her mother had left her a generation before. She finally divorced the children's father and has remarried. The boys live with their father and stepmother but spend weekends with their mother.

"I wondered what we might do from the distance of 500 miles to provide a feeling of belonging and continuity in the boys' lives," says Ellen. "After considerable thought, we bought an album of white pages encased in plastic and made computer-printed titles, "The Life of (boy's name) as Seen by Grandma and Grandpa Moore." Marty and I found great pleasure choosing pictures and composing captions about our special occasions when we were together. We emphasized the love in their lives. We also acknowledged the divorce the boys had experienced and included this sentence: 'It was sad for everybody.' I made sure to include several pictures of the boys with their mom.

"I counseled myself, 'Don't count on these books meaning as much to the children as you hope they will.' I need not have worried. Both accepted my request to sit beside them as they pored over each page, squealing and smiling at the shots that pleased them. The best thank you came when I peeked in at bedtime and found the five-year-old asleep with the album in his arms."

When an S.O.S. Arrives for a Long-Distance Grandparent

"Grandma, please come. Mom is driving me crazy," pleaded sixteen-year-old granddaughter Patty, from nearly 1,000 miles away in Washington State. Grandmother Delores, in Colorado, did her best to calm Patty, but made arrangements to leave her gift shop job long enough to visit and do what she could to calm the troubled waters for Patty and Delores' daughter, Pam.

Pam and Patty's father had been divorced for many years. The girl was close to her father and his new family and spent a lot of time with them, but she lived with her mother near the school she attended.

Pam had a live-in companion for a couple of years. Patty got along with him but when he suddenly left, "for greener pastures," says Delores. Pam was inconsolable.

"Mom cries all the time and she hardly speaks to me," Patty reported.

"A large part of the problem," says grandmother Delores, "was that the live-in had been paying half the mortgage. With his departure, Pam, on her salary, couldn't meet the monthly payments and keep food on the table as well. No wonder she was at her wit's end and abandoning her motherly duties."

Although Delores enjoyed her life in Boulder, she gave up her apartment and job there and moved in with the Washington daughter and granddaughter. She paid rent to help meet the mortgage expenses and will stay another year as a renter until Patty graduates from high school. Patty's birth father has promised to pay for her college education and by that time, Pam will be able to sell the heavily-mortgaged property and get more affordable housing nearer her job.

Delores has friends near her daughter and granddaughter where she once lived and is happy to do what she can to be of help to Pam and Patty, both financially and emotionally. After a couple of years she plans to return to the Boulder area and her many friends there. "We do what love and concern tells us to do," she says.

Grandparents Stand by as a Split Develops

"Our most troubling issue at the moment is the uncertainty of the parents' marriage," Sara reports. "There's talk of divorce. We are concerned about how the tension is affecting the grandkids and wonder how we can help mitigate effects and pick up the pieces, if separation comes to pass, all without sticking our noses in where they shouldn't be."

Grandfather Bert has already figured out how the boys would respond to the parents splitting up. "The twelve-year-old will just suck it up as the eldest child and hold his feelings in. The ten-year-old is more volatile and I'm concerned he'll become delinquent. The youngest will suffer a broken heart."

"I hope that Bert's prognosis does not come about," says Sara. "All we can do is be here for them, even though we're three hours driving distance away."

Grandparents taking sides can dynamite their relationship with the entire younger family, including the grandchildren. Maintaining a neutral position—*nobody is the bad guy*—is the most fruitful, as it encourages confidences from all parties. "When advice is asked, consider whether it supports the neutral position or seeks endorsement," says Sara.

Creating New Alliances after a Split

"Jack and I met twenty years ago," relates Nadine. "We were both in unhappy marriages at the time. After our respective divorces, we made the major decision to join forces. That was nineteen years ago, and from the first, we've been as close as blood parents to each other's children, and grandparents to each other's grandchildren, as surely as if the same genes moved through the blood streams of all.

"Now we have eighteen grandchildren between the ages of nine and twenty-five, and we are truly long-distance grandparents. The nearest are 200 miles away. None of these grandkids, except my oldest granddaughter, who was just five at our wedding, remembers a life when Jack and I were not married.

"Even though Jack's ex-wife forbade me to talk to any of her grandkids and threw insults my way in front of them, I managed never to hurl insults back. I cautioned myself that the children and grandchildren needed role models of proper behavior, and I did everything possible to be seen as that role model, loving, giving and building relationships with them.

"One of the ways Jack and I 'grandparent' is to prearrange one-on-one lunches with each grandchild, either when we visit them or they visit us. We take our charges to different restaurants so that each gets exclusive attention.

"What I have done most consistently is to baby-sit the grandkids when their parents go on vacation. When their parents are around, they don't need Gram and Gramps. But when the parents are away, grandparents car-pool them, help with homework, and advise on school science projects. We visit their exhibits and they know we love them and that they can count on us.

"I've shopped with my granddaughters, and given both girls and boys their first driving lessons. Jack teaches them to cook and helps them learn the uses of his workshop tools—saws, hammers, screwdrivers, planes, even the electric drill press and lathe. He makes gifts for them. A favorite is bird houses.

"We live in a beautiful area of Arizona and take them on hikes, individually or in small groups. I take them to the library or bookstore to find gems for them to read while visiting us, and keep a 'kid shelf' in my home library.

"When we discover that any one of them has a particular passion, we honor it.

"Framed grandkid art decorates the wall in my office, and a book of grandchild-authored poems sits on the shelf. The eldest grandson graduated from college last year and is now in Singapore. We had a great phone conversation this past holiday. In short, we love them all dearly—his and hers—equally."

Chapter 6

Grandfathers Are Special

Grandfathers have a unique position in the grandchild's life. Near or far, they are more important that they may realize.

More Participation than Talk

Grandfather Charles reports, "I make it a point to play with them and introduce them to places and activities they may not have a chance to know through their always-busy parents. I take them hiking, cycling, to parks and museums.

"Sometimes, distance makes the heart grow fonder. All grandparents face challenges as outside, concerned observers. How to suggest something or give advice without sticking your nose in? How to impart values, perhaps not fully available in the young family, without interfering? We do this by example, not by preaching. We also try to plug in to each child's distinct personality and interests.

"The grandkids always seem glad to see us. It's important to show how much we care about them through visits, phone calls, e-mails, and sending photos. When their grandmother and I visit, we try to trigger activities that will involve the whole family. During our last trip to their home, we went to a nearby park and played softball—mixed teams, adults and kids. All had fun. The six-year-old held his own with the adults. He even pitched!"

How-to Sharing

Although one set of grandkids lives nearby, most of Grandfather Charles' are 200 to 300 miles away. Dan likes to build things—especially model airplanes. He spends time talking on the phone with his grandsons about something they can work on when they are together.

"Apparently when the kids hit fourth or fifth grades they have to interview a family member about how things were in the 'olden' days," says Charles. "They seem to choose me more often than their grandmother. They can't believe I grew up without television. I tell them about radio programs in the 1930s and '40s—'Chandu, the Magician' and the 'Secret Door.' I imitate the sound of a squeaking door. They get a kick out of that. I tell them about the first car I drove, a Model T, and how it had to be cranked to start. It had running boards, isinglass windows and no seat belts. I get a lot of 'Wow, Gramps! Really?'

"The boys are involved in almost every sport—soccer, water polo, Little League, football, basket ball, volleyball. Whenever we visit them, we attend their sporting events. When I know what's coming up, I call to get the results of their matches.

"I think the most important thing about long distance grandparenting is communication. If you don't have e-mail, most kids have cell phones. If not cell phones, we can usually call in the evening by regular phone. Kids will talk if you get past the 'hello-how-are-you?-I-am-fine' litany. Concentrate on 'What did you do at school today? Do you like baseball or tennis better?'"

Hosting Grandkids on Trips

Earl reports about a long-distance visit with grandson Jimmy. "He is twelve and his school break falls in September. His parents are divorced and his grandmother, his aunts, and I tiptoe around bitterness and conflict between his estranged parents. Luckily, we have been able to maintain communication with his father, and our frequent-flyer miles bring Jimmy to us twice a year. The boy has had some tough times in his tender years, but he is brave and wise.

"Jimmy and I are firm pals, devoted more than anything else to the art of fishing. So the first day this year was spent out at the ponds near our home. Unfortunately, the fish weren't interested in the bait we offered, but his spirit was never dampened.

"We wanted to show him as much of the area as possible and took him to Estes Park to watch the elk wandering on private lawns and the golf course. This long trip brought us the unmistakable information that Jimmy is not fond of long drives. So the rest of the week was spent here at our home where he happily looked for frogs in a small lake behind the house. His biggest delight was reconstructing an old raft that he found. My blood pressure rose as I watched him pole around the lake, break loose from a mud bank in the middle and safely reach shore.

"A part of our treat for him was to return him to Oregon in our fifth wheel. We set out from Boulder in the rain, but found sunshine and a good camp on the western side of the Rockies. We were scarcely parked when the fishing poles came out and we were off to the lake. It was a good day except for the disinterest—again!—of the fish.

"The next morning was cold, but the determined little fisherman donned a hooded sweatshirt and grabbed a blanket, fishing pole, tackle box, a large net—just in case—and a folding chair. We headed for the lake shore.

"Jimmy is a good sport. Even though the fishing expeditions yielded no fish, he feels that trailer living is ideal. He helped daily with camp chores and found the perfect car game for long drives. He appropriated his grandmother's laptop, plugged it into the cigarette lighter, and watched the entire Harry Potter series with only a few naps in the back seat—and, of course, the occasional: 'How much farther? Just keep going, I want to get this over with.'

"The last of the bad weather caught us in a blizzard which delighted and awed Jimmy. We had planned the trip to include a visit to his mother in Nevada. Mother and son romped and rough-housed. They rode their bikes and promised to be together at his next school break.

"When we finally got him back to his father and stepmother, we were welcomed and invited to stay over Saturday to see his first baseball game of the season. Said his grandmother, 'No greater love hath grandparents than to sit through a baseball game in frigid rain.' But we saw our champion pitch, steal a run and end up being presented with the 'Ball of the Game.'"

Travel Games

Phil and his wife hosted their three grandchildren every summer. Their mother drove the kids from their California desert home to the grandparents Oregon Coast home so that the children could not only be with Gram and Gramps but also enjoy the cooler climate.

"Jessica, Audrey, and Kim loved to come and we had many wonderful activities together, mostly at the beach," says Phil. "When it was time to return, I drove them there and spent a little time with their mother, our youngest daughter, and her husband.

"It was a long trip. I don't know how their mother managed them in the car when she brought them, but they were certainly bored in the car with me. I couldn't endure the bickering: 'Grandpa, her legs are over on my side of the car.' 'She took my pillow.' 'She's looking at me!'

"To stifle this nonsense I invented a game based on Herbies—Volkswagen Beetles. I'd say, 'Count the Herbies. If you see ten between here and the next stop, I'll give you each a dollar.' This worked better than I expected because it forced them to concentrate on something besides each other. One watched out of one side of the car while the second watched the other side, and the third watched from the front seat beside me. Our rules allowed them to count parked, as well as moving, Herbies.

"This was a chance to give them money by having them 'earn' it. I don't believe in just handing over money. I worry that it gives the recipient a feeling that Grandpa is a never-ending source. At that time, Herbies were still fairly prevalent. I remember once being 'soaked' for five dollars each. As the girls matured, this became a standard event. Eventually we also counted the new Chrysler P.T. Cruiser. We had a lot of laughs out of this and they looked forward to the trip home. Now these girls are grown, the two eldest in college, and whenever we travel together, one is sure to spot an old Herbie.

"Another game we played in the car was Pick-a-State. Each girl chose a state whose license plate she would watch for. The one who identified the most states got five dollars at the end of the trip. Nobody was allowed to choose Oregon or California because those were the states we were traveling in."

Mishaps Happen!

Alvin writes, "One summer, my wife and I were caring for our four-year-old grandson and took him on a canoe ride in a nearby lagoon. When the wind came up, I knew we should get back but the waves were coming fast, and when we were within twenty-five yards of the shore, the canoe swamped. Martha grabbed grandson Tracy. I grabbed the canoe, which was just under the surface.

"Tracy wore a life jacket but kept trying to climb up on Martha's shoulders to get away from the water. I was afraid he was going to drown her. She later claimed that all she could think about was having to tell the boy's father how we came to drown his son. People in a motor boat saw our problem and sped to our rescue. The lagoon wasn't deep and I finally moved our canoe into shallow water. Our rescuers took Martha and Tracy to their trailer, dried his clothes and gave him a warm drink.

"We had 'waterproofed' our kids from the time they were little by teaching them to swim, and did not worry when they were around water. Before Tracy's father came for him we introduced the kid to water safety, and by the end of the summer he, like his father, was swimming like a fish."

Coastal Fun

An entirely different kind of entertainment was offered by grandparents Mort and Joy. "We lived near our two granddaughters, from birth to ages five and nine and we saw them two or three times a week," he reports. "When we moved to California's Central Coast it was a bit traumatic to keep in touch. The two girls came about every two months, and that was great. We did many wonderful, crazy things, hiking in the nearby coastal range, kayaking in the bay, running up and down the sand dunes, feeding the gulls from our hands, and visiting the elephant seals.

"A fun thing we did with them was to go out to Morro Rock, a landmark on the bay, for New Year's morning. We took blankets, coffee, and hot chocolate and watched the sun come up and the New Year come in."

Mort regularly led hikes to the Avila Bay Lighthouse. As soon as each granddaughter reached age twelve, she was permitted to go on the hike. This was a special goal that each aspired to. Now they are seventeen and twenty-one, and still recount these rites of passage with delight.

Mort loved the beach trips with granddaughters, as much fun for him as for the girls. "Beaches are where we created a 'frontier desert' or a 'pirate stronghold' to be warily explored and where rare jewels and relics could be gleaned. The first task was to prepare the shelter. We piled and laced together driftwood logs to become a frontier homestead. Once, the girls' plans called for a castle of about 2,000 square feet. My lack of endurance forced something a bit more manageable! Furnishing was next, and that's when the girls' search for jewels and relics became active, even competitive. They found sea shells, odd pieces of decorative wood, kelp floats, and fishing lures. Granddaughters' eyes and imaginations even found creativity in weeks-old 'horse apples'—horse droppings.

"As they grew older and outgrew hideaway construction on the beach and the performing of plays in our living room, they often visited separately. Now they come when they are free of job and school commitments. We still have wonderful times together. A lot of it is reminiscing."

Sand Sculpture

Mario, another grandfather, reports a special bond with his four granddaughters. Each summer the children, who live in a desert community in Arizona, arrive in California to spend off-school months with Gram and Gramps, who live within a mile of the sandy shore on the central coast.

Mario reports, "Granddaughter, Linda, is a fantastic artist and under her leadership, the family took first place in the local Fourth of July sand sculpture contest for five years running. Last year the Harbor Festival Committee asked the family to do a sand sculpture for $500. We agreed and arrived at 5:30 in the morning Saturday to find a truckload of dry sand that was supposed to have been placed in a board container and soaked.

"You cannot mold dry sand," Mario continues. "Linda grabbed a five gallon bucket and began hauling water from the bay to soak the sand. We searched the dock and found a hose to sprinkle the pile and asked a policeman if he could get the fire department to let us hook up to a fire plug nearby. He did, and we did. The four girls and I had our sculptures well started by then. Their creation was a huge bull seal with its head raised. Another lay on its side with a big smile on its face.

"These grandkids are talented and creative. Once when the two older ones were eight and five, they were bored. I suggested they do some figure painting on rocks they'd found on the shore. These rocks were smooth and light-colored. The children spent a week decorating them. Although ours is a residential street, it is a busy one. The girls set up a card table in our driveway and sold their arty rocks. In two three-hour stints they made over $200.

"This quickly became their regular summer business. When the two younger girls were old enough, they got to join in as rock-art purveyors. I still have painted rocks stored in one of the cabinets. Now when the grown girls visit, we have a great time reviewing memories of their rock art business."

Although Mario's grandchildren are creative, his support and encouragement have obviously been a key to their sand sculpture winnings, and their entrepreneurial endeavors.

Fishy Business

Albert is another grandfather who lives near the Pacific. He regularly shares summer fun with his visiting grandson Len and granddaughter Kit. "Grandkids are really good for grandparents. They keep you on your toes with unending questions. I spend lots of time looking up stuff to be sure they get the right answers.

"Crab fishing is Len's favorite. It requires special equipment. We use a hoop about thirty-six inches across and fix a net to it. Len helps me tie fish carcasses to the netting and we lower the hoop and net on a rope. After about twenty minutes, we pull the net up. We used to get up to thirty crabs in one net and we'd keep only three or four of the biggest out of each pull. Now we are lucky to pull up four or five.

"Len can't wait to pull the net. If we pull up a starfish, which is often, the kid stops the tourists who are walking on the pier to show them the eyes at the end of each leg. He lets other kids hold them before we return them to the sea. Sometimes we pull in an octopus.

"I've taught Len and Kit as much as I can about respect for the sea creatures. They have been pinched by a few crabs and Kit has been nipped by an octopus. But these kids are generally fearless and these incidents do nothing to quell their enthusiasm. They're often the information sources for adults as well as their contemporaries. Back home with the crabs, the grandkids help crack the claws and extract the delicious meat so Grandma can make crab cakes."

Salmon Eggs

Gordon's grandson visits him each year at his mountain cabin on the Upper Klamath River in Oregon. They hike the trails together, watching for deer and an occasional bobcat. But the most treasured adventure has been going down to the river when the salmon come to spawn. Watching the female salmon use their tails to dig the gravel nest and lay eggs has been a source of wonder for both Gordon and the boy. "He wrote a paper for his sixth grade class about our adventures," says Gordon. "The wonders of nature fascinate most kids if you just take them out into the mountain country and let them see wildlife for themselves."

Rock Painters

Martin and his wife, Shirley, live in rural Arizona. He is "Mister Outdoors," a hiker, amateur archeologist, and student of Indian lore. Their grandkids—two in each family—come two at a time. The four range in age from seven to twelve, two boys and two girls. Martin has made walking sticks from natural wood found on their rural property. Each child, "carefully supervised," says Martin, has carved his initials on his stick that is stored with Grandpa's hiking gear and joyfully retrieved as the young guests arrive.

"We take them during the day to the Palatki Indian Ruins where pictographs, [symbols painted on the rock faces] and pueblo ruins are the main attractions.

"We also visit an archeology site, famous for its petroglyphs [incised symbols on rock].

"Docents at both sites recite histories and mysteries of the ancient people who created the rock art and the pueblos. We provide notebooks so the kids can sketch the symbols they see on the rock faces.

"The *coup de grace,*" says Martin, "comes in the evening when our guests become rock artists. Their tools are a box of acrylic paints from Wal-Mart and a few yucca leaves from our back yard. I help them cut the leaves into six-inch sections and pound the ends with a blunt rock or hammer to expose the fibers. After scraping excess pulp from the fibers, our young people are impressed that the result is a small paintbrush made the way the ancient rock artists made theirs.

"When our young artists are ready to paint, we have them select their colors and choose their subjects from the images they copied from the pictographs and petroglyphs. Their canvases are small, flat red rocks abundant in our area. Once the painting begins, all become 'Puebloan Picassos.' They are completely absorbed in the process which can take as many hours as we have rocks.

"The end result is a souvenir paper weight or simply a keepsake that the young artist is able to take home. This is an offering of entertainment that never fails," says Martin. "Of course, each set of kids arrives only once a year. I'm not sure how this entertainment would go over if it were offered on a daily basis. I also take them on bicycle rides and let them help me when I gather water samples for Friends of the Forest."

Mixed Loyalties

Nevada-based grandparents Cliff and Marie have formed a long and happy relationship with each other. But they are not married. Both are grandparents. She has four direct-descendent grandkids and Cliff has six. One of Cliff's sons and his wife, both fundamentalist ministers, live in Montana. Since Cliff and Marie are not married, these adult children refuse to acknowledge that Marie exists.

Marie says, "I used to send cards, especially when one baby died, and little gifts for the other children, but none was ever acknowledged."

Cliff writes nature and family life stories for the local newspaper and sends copies to the Montana children and grandchildren between his visits to them. The last time he was there, he found a note on his pillow from his eight-year-old granddaughter. She begged him to accept Jesus Christ as his Savior because they told her at school that anyone who didn't could not go to Heaven, and she couldn't bear for him not to be there with her.

Cliff thanked her warmly for her message and her concern. Back home he wrote a letter to her to say that she should not worry about this now, that when she's older, he will explain his ideas to her.

"That may not be the best response," says Cliff. "I am overwhelmed by her concern. But my message to her avoids for now my offering ideas that are incompatible with teachings of her parents. Any words that counter their philosophy would cause the child as much distress as worrying about Grandpa's eventual destination in Hell."

The long-distance communication, the one-on-one experiences, are different for each family, each set of grandparent and each grandkid. We learn from each other by sharing our experiences, our questions, and our concerns.

Chapter 7

Postal Communication

Pictures Worth Thousands of Words

Katherine's granddaughter Jody is too young to come for a visit, unless it's with her parents. The young family lives more than 500 miles away. "We do talk on the phone, but little kids don't like to sit and chat with Nana about what they're doing because they want *to be doing it,*" Katherine says. "Jody and I share a love of cats and kittens. Almost every magazine that comes into my home has pictures of animals. I clip all the pretty kitties and mail them to her. Sometimes I write a little note that pretends it's from the kitten whose picture I send. I give the cat a name and this delights her. She loves to get mail."

"My step-grandchild Peter is fourteen," says Loraine. I've been married to his grandfather since the boy was seven. His parents are separated, but I think his mother has done a fabulous job of raising him. He and I have bonded over a mutual love of nature. I send him cards and information about animals that I think he might like. I get to see him once or twice a year and we always have good conversations. He thinks of me more as a friend than a grandmother and calls me 'Auntie-Gram.' Last fall, I found yellow, orange and red leaves in our back yard and mailed them to him. His response by letter: 'Gee, Auntie-Gram, you think of cool things to send in envelopes.'"

Mail–More Affordable than Airfare

"I don't see my grandkids as often as I would like because the distance between us is so great and I'm still employed," reports Anne of South Carolina. "The children and grandkids live in Wyoming. So I write letters to them that I hope they will treasure when they get older. I remind them of games that we have played together, the words they were saying at the time, where they were living when I saw them last, what their mom and dad were doing at the time, and what pets they had. Even if they do not read them now, they'll have these letters. Their parents thank me for preserving these records of the kids' childhood and they're preserving my letters in scrapbooks."

Dual Loyalties for Grandma

"I do not have funds to fly from Colorado to California where my grandson, Arnold, lives," says Angie. "He is eleven. I write to him about my life here where I live with his uncle, aunt, and girl cousin, Petra, exactly his age. I'm a live-in grandma/sitter/transportation provider for Petra, while her parents work. I tell Arny about the art projects that Petra and I do together and her girlfriends' sleepovers. I always enclose a five-dollar bill in my monthly letters to him to let him know I am thinking of him and love him. I'm gratified that he telephones to thank me. In these ways, letter and phone, we have a little one-on-one relationship that is just our own."

Zero in on the Child's Interests

New Mexico-based grandparents Muriel and Hank write lots of letters to the Maine-based grandkids. "Address them to the child, not the parent," advises Muriel. "I always ask the kids what they are studying in school. If it's Indians, I'll send information from a newspaper or magazine. If it is European history, I tell them about our experiences living in France after World War II. Kids love to get mail and this may be the only mail they receive.

"Of course, birthdays, Christmas, Easter and Halloween are times for mailing greeting cards," adds Muriel. "We save any colorful greeting cards that come in and when the grandkids visit, I lay out scissors, glue, and blank cards. They cut images from the cards and glue them to the blanks. These become their own creations that they mail to friends and family."

Grandkids Scattered across the Continents

Rosa and Jose live in Florida. Their grandkids range in age from seven to twenty-five. The eldest was wounded in the service but is home in West Virginia. He's scheduled to visit the grandparents over the holidays. Two grandkids, ages fifteen and eighteen, live with their parents on missionary duties in North Africa. One grandson in Maine is soon to become a doctor. "He has little time for communicating with anybody," says Rosa. "And our youngest grandson lives in California. We're spread out so far that personal visits are infrequent. Letters are the only way we can stay in touch. I write or e-mail everyone about once a month. I ask about their school schedules and which classes they like best. When I send letters, I always include a self-addressed, stamped envelope for replies. We also send checks for birthdays and holidays."

Mail across the Seas

Roberta, now a resident of Indiana, is the mother of four, the grandmother of ten and great grandmother of thirteen. Her family is scattered across the U.S. When two of her grandchildren, Sally and Darrel, were three and five, their parents moved to Germany and lived there several years, as their father was in the military.

"I was saddened by this." Roberta says. "How could the little ones know their grandparents without seeing or talking to us? They did not even have a telephone. I was desperate and devised a plan.

"In the beginning I bought each child a bright colored, loose-leaf notebook and wrote all my letters on notebook paper, so they could be preserved.

"I wrote three letters every Monday morning: one to the parents, one to Darrel, and one to Sally. I made up little stories with names of pretend boys Darrel's age, beginning with the first letter of the alphabet. For instance, *'Hello. Darrel, My name is Adam. I am five years old and I sure like apples. Do you ever see apple trees? I pick them at my grandma's farm. Your grandparents like apples too and your Grandma makes wonderful apple pies. They love you and want you to see what you can find out about apples. Your friend, Adam.'* The next letter was from 'a new friend,' whose name began with the letter B. And so on, through the alphabet. It took two weeks for the letters to arrive in Germany. Sending those messages filled a year of Mondays for me.

"The next year I did the same thing using careers and vocations as topics that each pretend 'alphabetical child' wrote. I spent many hours with books as I searched for ideas. I bought little gifts that related to the alphabet letters. With stencils I put the letter of the alphabet on each message, then colored it, and found pictures from magazines to illustrate.

"The letters to Sally came from an idea in a quilting magazine. I made up a family of four Sunbonnet girls. Each week, for three years, these fictional Sunbonnet girls did something different. Little Sally fell in love with the imaginary characters, and when the family retuned to the U.S. she begged me to make her a sunbonnet. I did, of course, and also made clothes for her doll.

"Darrel is now twenty-six and comes to see me every week. We eat lunch or dinner together and he does any chores I need taken care of. Sally is away with her husband, who is in the army. So I continue to write lots of letters. Cards are nice. I send 400 to 500 each year. But the children, grandkids, and great-grandkids seem to like the letters better.

"Do anything to keep in touch. I love writing letters and got the start, of course, with wanting to know and be known by those tots who were away in Germany so long ago."

Distance and Language Barriers

"Our long-distance grandparenting has been a bit complicated by the international, bilingual aspect of the relationship," says Arlene in Southern California. "I can't think of anything super-original that we've done. We send the kids pictures of us, so they can remember what we look like between visits. I've also found tapes of nursery songs in both French and English. My heart feels sorry that these French-speaking grandkids won't know many Mother Goose rhymes. I've tried to teach them but haven't spent enough personal time with them for old nursery rhymes to take hold.

"We have made tapes of ourselves reading stories, and sent the books and a child's tape player. We also send presents for birthdays and Christmas, trying to choose things that appeal to their hobbies. We telephone often. We used to visit them twice a year in Switzerland, but have cut it back to once. Nothing beats the memories of holidays spent together.

"When we visit, we stay in a small apartment at a village inn near our children's home as they do not have room in their house for us. We often invite them all for meals in our little rented apartment. The youngest grandchild once asked her mother, as they walked past the inn, why Grandma and Grandpa did not invite them more often. She thought we lived there and were available only on rare occasions.

"The nine-year-old granddaughter loved the American doll we sent, so now we know that the doll clothes are welcome presents. These come with story books about American history. She is managing to read some English as does the eleven-year-old. These kids know us quite well, and seem happy to see us. Even though we haven't been too original in our contacts, we are making headway."

Mail Service Working Wonders

Lorry and Martin live in Hawaii, but they return to California each year for several months to visit children and grandchildren. "For years, since the grandkids were born, we have sent a smiling picture of ourselves with each birthday and holiday gift. If the child is very young he soon forgets, and, of course, we 'aging ones' change in appearance just as they do. We often send small gifts rather than big things.

"Really, it is up to us, the grandparents, to be as much a part of the grandchildren's lives as we choose. Inevitably their lives are filled with growing up. We need to face the fact that unless we keep in touch, and spend enough real time with them to bond, they are not likely to remember us or to try to keep in touch.

"We send newspaper clippings about the Hawaiian volcanoes, but assure them that we are far away from such potential disasters. These make interesting reading for the nine- and ten-year-olds, and the volcano eruptions make them anxious to come to visit us in Hawaii.

"Their parents finally told us to stop sending savings banks. They were too much trouble for the parents when the kids insisted they needed some of the coins. *To break or not to break the banks?*

"When we send cards with a substantial amount of money earmarked for school, it means a trip to the bank for the parent, but that becomes a real help later on. In general we've learned that a $500 check for a birthday might not end up in the college fund where we intended it to be. Instead, we have purchased certificates of deposit that we add to from time to time and let the child know how his savings account is growing.

"Basically, we do what our hearts tell us while we are still here to do it."

Postcards Launch a Hobby

Valerie, another long-distance grandparent, is a life-long antique collector. Among her treasures are old postcards.

"From age three when my grandson came to visit, he would be

entertained for an hour or more with my box of old buttons. He examined every one carefully and sorted them into piles by color or size or material. Then I began to collect old postcards and thought Tommy would enjoy them. I have several boxes of these that I take to our postcard club meetings. When I last visited the family, Tommy was five. I took along my boxes of postcards, showed them to him and suggested that he stack together all the ones that showed cars, or people, or streams and lakes. This was highly successful. While his mother and I visited and prepared dinner, he spent hours happily rearranging all my cards.

"Recently our club received a donation of about six boxes of advertising rack cards. These are created specifically for young people, eighteen to thirty, and placed free on college campuses, in bars, cafes, music and video stores. They are 'arty' and bright, and often feature TV and movie stars, and cartoon characters.

"Tommy loved the advertising rack cards and asked me for his own official postcard storage box which I happily provided. Now I regularly mail cards to him. He loves the ones showing animals or cartoon figures. Sometimes I send several in the same week. But I am selective.

"Last week I drove again to visit the family in Santa Fe and we attended an antique show together. Tommy and I sat looking though a box of old postcards for sale. I told him he could pick six. It took him more than an hour to choose. This promises to be an ongoing hobby for Tommy and has provided a strong bond between us."

Postcards Teach Geography

Here's another postcard story. It comes from Grandfather Donald, who launched a geography lesson for visiting grandson Carl. He showed Carl his collection of postcards. These were regulation, one-cent, government-issue postcards available in the 1940s and '50s. As a boy, his curiosity about the location of small towns scattered across the country led him to develop a system of sending a self-addressed postcard in an envelope addressed to "Postmaster" in small towns with unusual names that he found on a map of the U.S. He received his postcards back with cancellation records from hundreds of these little towns.

The last time Carl visited, Don asked him to help organize these. He provided a map of the U.S. and the box of postage canceled cards. Carl spent hours organizing the cards by states "And he learned a lot of U.S. geography as he sorted them," says Don.

Photo Postage Stamps

Grandparents Marylou and Bill encourage letter writing with their Michigan-based grandchildren, by converting individual photos of granddaughter Gloria and her brother Michael to authentic postage stamps. They sent blocks of these first-class photo stamps as gifts for birthdays and Christmas.

"This new service provided by the U.S. Postal Service has elicited prompt and cordial letters of response, enhancing the letter writing skills and proclivities of the grandkids," says Bill.

It's also possible to purchase postage stamps that feature the symbol of a grandchild's favorite football team or NASCAR driver— even a favorite college or university. "Get the college student grandchildren to correspond more often by gifting them with stamps that represent the schools they are attending," Bill adds.

Chapter 8

Cyberspace to the Rescue

In the "dark days" before computers took over our lives, some of us grandparents remember a rumor that "soon" we would be able to see the person we were calling on the telephone, and that person could see us! Several of us, then mothers, not grandparents, discussed this at social gatherings and most agreed that it might cause problems. "I wouldn't want to have to comb my hair and put on lipstick before I answer the phone!" exclaimed one concerned mother.

Times have changed. Have you noticed? With e-mail, chat rooms, cell phones and webcams, communication has taken us into outer space, and we don't mean a trip to Mars or the Moon.

Homework Hotline

Suzanne lives in Henderson, Nevada. She has always had a special bond with grandchild Mina in Placerville, California. Throughout Mina's elementary and junior high school days, e-mail became their main communication. However, the exchange wasn't as much news of "what's going on here" as it was requests for help with homework.

"Mina faxed me her completed math problems," reports Suzanne. "I marked the ones she got wrong and faxed her tips, where appropriate, but never the correct answer. This exchange also worked well for reports and stories. I line-edited, to some extent, and always tried to add comments that would provoke more thought on her part. The hardest thing was making her understand that I needed enough lead time so that I wouldn't get a ten-page fax at 9 P.M., when the paper was due the next morning."

They also did spelling tests by phone. "I often dictated a word and Mina wrote it down and spelled it back to me."

This kind of cyberspace and phone communication kept their relationship alive and was welcomed by Mina's parents as well keeping the "hot-liners" in close communication.

These days e-mail is a standard on most computers. It provides near-instant communication. The Internet, of which e-mail is a part, offers a tremendous array of answers to virtually any question or subject you and/or your grandchildren are interested in. Google, a "search engine," is a tool that can lead you to information on nearly any subject. The name "Google" has even become a verb. "Just google it and you'll find more answers than you need," we often hear in answer to an inquiry.

Most communities have free or low cost classes to teach computer skills. Check with your local adult center, high school, or community college if you aren't computer savvy yet.

Chat Rooms and Instant Messaging

The chat room programs bring a small box up on the computer screen of both sender and receiver so two can "talk" back and forth with their fingers dancing over the keys.

Instant messaging works like a chat room. You can chat with one person or you can use it to chat with a group of people. Bess, who lives on Long Island, "cyber chats" with her grandchildren in Israel and Canada.

Small cameras, costing about fifty dollars or less, can be attached to the computer so grandparents and grandchildren can see *and* speak to each other. This facility evolved when corporations required meetings of all board members, even though they were physically located miles apart.

CDs, Videos, Tapes

Grandmother Beverly makes a CD or video of herself reading a book to a child when she visits them or they visit her. She sends a copy of the book to the child along with the video.

In another use of the video, she reads and displays pictures of javelinas, tarantulas, and coyotes that roam near her desert home. These are creatures the children do not see in their city home in Massachusetts.

Beverly has seven grandchildren, three now in their early teens. She inquires by phone as to which books they are reading, then checks them out of her library to read. She e-mails questions and suggestions back and forth, keeping her in close touch with the progress of these young folks, mainly letting them know that she cares.

Whether or Not They Respond

Here is a somewhat different evaluation of the same problem of distance. "Our two sons live in Indiana, a long way from our Texas home," says Grayson. "We visit them every two years, and I talk to them by phone monthly and e-mail weekly. Occasionally, I e-mail the grandchildren. My son gives them the messages but they do not write back.

"Except once. There was this exception: I wrote a long e-mail to the grandson who was beginning to use the computer and was involved in Little League baseball. I asked a lot of questions—the position he played, where they played, was it near home, etc. I closed with the question, 'Is it lots of fun for you?' I received a one-word, e-mailed response: 'Yes'.

"We are now in a position to travel more and will see these grandkids more often. We look forward to the time when they will be old enough to visit us on their own. My advice to other grandparents is to begin communicating when they are very young and don't stop just because they don't respond in some way. As adults, supposedly more wise, we must recognize that long distance grandparenting is difficult for the grandkids to grasp. It may take a while before they truly recognize the significance of absentee grandparents."

Creating a Story Together

Bonnie hit on a unique idea using e-mail. She suggested to grandson Daniel that they write a story together. She wrote the first paragraph of a mystery and asked Daniel to compose the second paragraph or scene. They go back and forth writing a story this way.

For instance, she started a story (borrowing the universal interest in the Harry Potter series) and titled it: *How To Catch a Wizard*. She launched the tale by introducing a character, Willy Wizard: "Willy Wizard knew that he could work his magic to fly from his hideaway to Melloland. But he also knew that Daniel was expecting to find him there and might wait to ambush him and steal his magic baton."

Bonnie invited Daniel to write the next paragraph. He did, and the story took shape. "We had fun and eventually came up with a rollicking tale about how Daniel chased the Willy Wizard on his bicycle and grabbed the magic baton. It didn't make much sense, but Daniel and I kept the e-mail flying and his imagination soaring."

Communication in Verse

Frances tells of a similar project. "When my granddaughter and I last saw each other at her home, I took an old book of nursery rhymes. I had read these rhymes to Marilee's mother when she was little. Among them was *Humpty Dumpty Sat On A Wall* and *Hey Diddle, Diddle, The Cat and The Fiddle*.

"At age seven Marilee is already quite adept at using e-mail," says Frances. "I suggested that I write two lines that rhymed and e-mail them to her. She was to write two more rhyming lines. Under the title 'Love You, Marilee' my two lines were:

I know a little girl, her name is Marilee,
I love her and I hope that she loves me.
This inspired the grandchild to write:
I know Marilee and she knows you
She is making this poem so she won't feel blue.

"This exchange went on for several weeks and we wound up with a twenty-line verse. It wasn't Emily Dickinson, but it was fun and it bridged the long distance between us with warm communication and learning."

E-Mail Not for All

"I'm stuck in the typewriter age," says Grandma Sue. "I know I could probably increase communication with the grandkids—and their parents—if I got a computer and learned how to use it. But it just seems more effort than I want to put out. In the time it would take me to buy the right computer, go to the adult center and take a series of classes, I could type, or hand-write, lots of letters. I felt somewhat redeemed a few days ago when I received a thank you note from my grandson in college. He wrote:

Dear Gram, that $25 check came at exactly the right time. I needed a new chemistry book for my class. It saves me having to walk to the library and we're having 40-degree weather here now. Besides, seeing your hand-written letter brings you closer. Thank you, Josh."

Even though Grandfather David is skilled in the use of the computer and e-mail, he feels, like Sue, that correspondence by "snail mail" is a value to the grandchild and preserves family history in a more tangible way. He sends hand-written letters to his nine-year-old grandson in a distant city. They cover all manner of topics. David usually writes about nature, photography and his sculpturing projects. Fred writes about his school activities and interests. "Our letters," says Grandfather David, "are treasures to keep—so different from 'plain vanilla' e-mails."

Chapter 9
Grandparents Recall Their Grandparents

Little Red's Visit to Grandmother

We all know what Little Red Riding Hood discovered after walking through the woods to Grandmother's house. And, we are grateful to report that none of the grandparents interviewed for this book donned wolf's clothing and masks to welcome their grandchildren. Many traveled long distances to visit their grandparents. They loved and savored those trips and savor them even today. Here are a few.

Though times have changed drastically in the past fifty years, these ideas and experiences may be of use for today's long distance grandparents. Whatever you as a grandparent offer, as the host or the visitor, the location and performance of all parties will require ever-changing responses. We must be flexible.

Endless Adventure at Grandma's

Each summer shortly after school let out, my sisters and I—country kids all—rode in a Model A Ford, driven by my mother, the 250 miles to Grandmother's home in the city. Fontana was not really a city but a suburb of San Bernardino, a metropolitan area in Southern California. Grandmother's "city," however, was much larger than our little ranch town. For us, the two-week visit was extraordinary in all ways.

The first neat thing we did was to don our bathing suits and run through the sprinklers on grandmother's lawn. Our ranch had alfalfa fields but no lawns. My boy cousin, a year older than I, usually went with us. Sometimes he disconnected the sprinkler head from the hose and squirted us girls with a hard stream of water. This brought squeals of delight from us and a quick appearance of grandmother on the front porch to order the sprinkler head reattached so the water would not puddle on the lawn.

The most enchanting contact with water came when we walked to the civic center, five blocks away, to splash and swim in the public swimming pool. We could stay all afternoon–for a dime. Our little town had no public swimming pool.

Today many children cannot safely walk several blocks to a city swimming pool. But swimming and diving lessons are available in most cities and excellent ways for grandparents to entertain visiting grandchildren.

Secret Hideaway

The most intriguing feature of grandmother's property was an unoccupied apartment above the garage, at the end of the driveway. The apartment was sparsely furnished and smelled of dust and mold. Spooky! We were allowed to imagine it as any fanciful abode we wished. The long, outside staircase leading up to the apartment became the steps to a princess' castle. Grandmother taught us to braid. We braided ropes from heavy cord. We dangled the ropes over edge of the staircase landing to become Rapunzel's hair so the prince could climb up.

Gathering Eggs

Grandmother raised White Leghorn chickens. A daily chore was to help gather eggs that were sold to a local broker. Even though

I broke a few, Grandma never scolded. At home on the ranch, a motley group of hens produced a few eggs in random nests. If I dropped one in the gathering process, it meant I didn't get my egg for breakfast the next morning.

Grandmother also had three acres of navel orange trees that were harvested by the time summer came. We loved the trees for climbing. What adventures! Low branches enabled us to swing up and straddle a limb. We imagined ourselves to be Tom Mix or Tex Ritter, galloping across the prairie. At home, the locust trees offered no low branches to climb.

All the World's a Stage

My grandmother's living room was larger than ours. She let us rearrange furniture to create a stage for plays. We pulled the sofa away from the wall so that the hero in our mysteries could disappear. He escaped by jumping up on the couch and dropping behind it. Grandmother was our faithful audience and applauded every performance.

Above all, she read to us–grown up stories–from the *Saturday Evening Post*. That was my favorite special treat and set the stage for my becoming a writer.

Stilts and HO Trains

Eileen remembers visiting grandparents who introduced her to stilts. These were long, slender boards that Grandpa tapered at the top for hand-holds. He nailed a block of wood several inches up from the bottom to create the foot platform. He steadied her until she mastered walking across the driveway and the lawn.

"The stilts elevated me no more than fifteen inches above the ground, but I felt as tall as a giant," she says. Grandpa made her another kind of stilts. "These were large, empty coffee cans. He drilled holes on opposite edges of the bottoms of the cans, threaded heavy cord through the holes, and knotted both ends on the inside to create a loop. We would put our feet on the bottom of the can between the cord ends and pull up on the loop to keep each foot tight against the can. This resulted in a few bruises, but it was lots of fun."

The year Eileen's younger brothers came with her to the grandparents' country home, Grandpa converted the cellar into a setting for an HO model railroad train complete with station. Christmas time brought the requisite HO engine, four cars, and a caboose. When the three children arrived the next summer, they placed small buildings and signs in the setting and ran the train on the track.

Popping Good Fun

A favorite treat for Maria and Sam when they visited Grandma was scattering popcorn kernels on the top of her woodburning stove in the kitchen. "We made a game of catching the fluffy white popped corn in our mouths," says Maria. "Grandma laughed with us and said that the mice would clean up what we didn't catch. I know this caused her extra sweeping. It was a farm kitchen and mice were a nuisance. Even the resident cats couldn't catch all of them."

Castle in a Closet

Audra reports that whenever she and her sister visited Grandma in the city, the front hall closet had been cleared. "I don't know where she stored the canes and overcoats and galoshes that were usually kept there," she says. "But Christy and I found the card table, always kept in the hallway. We set it up in front of the open closet door and covered it with a blanket. The space beneath the table and the closet opening combined to provide us a castle to hide in or rooms to play house with our dolls. Grandma provided a pad on the closet floor. She kept art materials and tiny play dishes there. Odd-shaped empty boxes became chairs and tables for our dolls. We gathered leaves from the maple tree in the front yard for plates and acorn caps form beneath the oak tree to serve as tea cups for our dolls."

Grandparents in a Different World

"From the time I was a year old until I reached eighteen, I spent my summers with my grandparents, Nana and Poppop, in rural Kansas," reports Alice. "My mother and I drove from our East Coast home to this wonderland. It was a totally different culture than we knew in the New York suburbs. My father, an attorney, could not take the whole summer with us, but he did visit for short periods. Mother was a teacher so she had summers off.

"One of my most vivid and enjoyable memories is sitting on the front porch every evening in the porch swing, moving back and forth to cool ourselves in the hot Kansas air. We chatted together and waved to the neighbors across the street or those who paused at the gate as they took an evening stroll.

"Laundry at Nana's was done in big galvanized tubs that sat in the backyard. The hot water tub was for washing, the cold water one for rinsing. I liked washing but when I grew tall enough to reach the line I loved hanging the laundry. I'd hang sheets and towels and pin them with wooden peg clothespins. After the wash was done, we carried the tubs to the flower garden to water Nana's fabulous lilies, phlox and roses.

"Once each summer, we went into the countryside to pick wild elderberries, clusters of tiny bluish-purple fruit. I helped wash them and watched as Nana made elderberry jelly. She taught me to make dill pickles and bread and butter pickles from homegrown cucumbers. On special occasions, she made cream puffs and let me fill them with whipped cream.

"Nana had been a nurse and homemaker and was an accomplished seamstress. She sewed clothes for me and for my dolls, and taught me how to use her treadle Singer sewing machine. I made my first skirts and aprons under her watchful eye.

"On Saturday nights we dressed up to go downtown, three blocks of small-town America. It seemed like everybody went there on Saturday night, to the picture show or to stores to check out the latest wares. It was a big social event and, as I reached my teens, I always watched for whichever boy I had a crush on at the time.

"Back home in New York, we received penny postcards daily from Nana. My mother saved every one of these, secured by ribbons, and labeled by years. Nana wrote in pencil and, surprisingly, the writing has not faded. I still have them and read them from time to time. They are very precious to me, along with photos of my grandparents that hang in my home."

Whether Alice's good memories derive more from the pleasures and curiosities of rural life or the loving support of her Nana and Poppop is immaterial. What is certain is that our grandkids today will learn and profit from any circumstances or locations to which we can introduce them—anything different from what they experience in their day-to-day lives.

Chapter 10

Educational-Recreational Intergenerational Tours

There are numerous opportunities to share an adventure with your grandchildren. (See the resources section at the back of this book for contact information for some of these organizations.)

Rankin Ranch

Rachel reports on a great place for grandparents, parents, and children to vacation at the same time. "Originally a cattle ranch, Rankin Ranch lies in the Tehachapi mountains above Bakersfield, California, not far from my home. When cattleman Rankin died, we all thought his widow would give up and sell the place. But she stayed on, running the ranch on her own, until she turned part of it into a resort/guest ranch. It is beautiful and the staff is great. Reservations for people who are not long-time regulars must be made long in advance. People come all the way from Europe to experience the Rankin Ranch."

Rachel has been taking her children and grandchildren there for years. The ranch hands take the children over completely, offering horseback riding, hay wagon rides, fishing, hiking, and up-close-

and-personal encounters with farm animals. The parents and grand-parents are free to kick back, read, and enjoy each other while the children have a ball. The kids even eat at tables separate from the adults.

"There are never any discipline problems because there is so much for the kids to do and talk about over dinners," says Rachel. "Sometimes the children perform for the adults. This was my grandchildren's favorite because they got to wear costumes and makeup.

"The facilities are old and gracious. Part of the charm of the ranch is its history. It's expensive, but I save for it and the parents chip in. We reserve every other year or so, and all enjoy it."

Intergenerational Travel–Increasingly Available

Adrianne, another long-distance grandmother who lives on the West Coast, reports that the rest of her family who live on East Coast decided that this year they should stage an all-family bonding vacation for six adults and four children. The chosen destination was Turks and Caicos, an all-inclusive family resort about 575 miles off the coast of Florida.

"The family told me that they would not accept 'no' for an answer. I'd had recent lung surgery and recovered well, but I suspected they wanted us all together 'before it's too late.' By today's standards we are all still young. Our ages range from two to sixty-two. I'm self-employed and my work is pressing but I always feel we have a choice every morning when we wake up: to make it a positive or negative day. So I agreed to meet them for this adventure. The resort stresses intergenerational entertainment.

"Included were food, drinks, room, and transport to and from the airport. It was like Sesame Street came off the screen for the kids. Cartoon characters roamed the grounds providing lots of photo opportunities. We enjoyed stage performances, games and enter-tainment. The resort also offers baby sitting, crafts classes, water sports, playgrounds, a beautiful white sand beach, snorkeling, scuba diving, and a submarine-type adventure. It turned out very well, and my daughter and her husband were right. We needed this time together, as there had been some misunderstandings among a few family members."

Deana writes, "The most rewarding endeavor I have had is to take each one of my twelve grandchildren—ranging in age from nine to twenty-eight—on an intergenerational trip, each about two weeks long. For most of them I have aimed at age thirteen because, by then, they are old enough not to be homesick and they really get something substantive out of the trip. And, at this age, they're still young enough to be manageable. So far I've made ten trips: New York, Alaska, and to far flung destinations including Kenya and Australia. Admittedly, most of these trips have been quite expensive and part of that is because of the company I choose to travel with.

"I have nothing but lavish praise for Grandtravel, headquartered in Washington, D.C. The head of the company is a grandmother herself, and every trip has been a winner. Their domestic trips are more affordable.

"Increasingly, I have discovered other options. Many college alumni travel programs include 'family' adventures. So far I've traveled with Stanford University and Interhostel through the University of New Hampshire. The latter offered a Harry Potter trip to the British Isles. My grandson adored that. It was actually less expensive than the more distant trips.

"Last year, the eligible grandson—and I!—wanted to go to Machu Picchu more than anywhere. He found a trip he felt was best, and I give him credit for doing a great job. In fewer than two weeks, we not only made it to Machu Picchu and the Amazon jungle but also to the Galapagos Islands. The company was Great Adventure People, based in Canada. It was promoted as a family trip and we had a marvelous time. But it nearly did me in. Although the term 'moderate' described the difficulty, it was the pacing that was exhausting—late to bed, early to rise. Of course, I was more than twenty years older than anyone else on the trip. So, caution is the watchword.

"Anyway, I feel I've been privileged to have a special time with each grandchild. Two more to go, but I have four summers off to rest up, which I feel I need after Peru. Going with these intergenerational groups has a decided advantage. The poor kid isn't stuck with Grandma as his only company."

Within the past twenty-five years, a number of travel organizations have begun to schedule domestic and worldwide trips for grandparents and their grandchildren.

Elderhostel Programs

The following information is quoted from the current Elderhostel catalog:

> Elderhostel, a not-for-profit travel organization founded in 1975, began offering intergenerational trips throughout the world the following year. The organization provides more than 8,000 educational programs in all 50 states and in more than 90 countries worldwide. These are conducted by experienced program leaders and the best local experts. Such experiences strengthen relationships, forge new bonds, and build bridges of understanding between generations. Some programs can accommodate three generations. As a bonus, many programs discount prices for young participants.

A typical U.S. experience for Elderhostelers and young learners—the recommended age range is listed with the description of every trip—is a five-day visit to Yellowstone National Park. The description includes the following information:

> This Intergenerational program is for Elderhostelers and young learners ages 8–11. One youth per adult in shared accommodations. Lodgings and activities at elevations of 6,600 to 7,000 ft. Hikes of approximately two miles on boardwalks, asphalt paths, stairs and trails; moderately steep and rocky trail to Geyser Hill. Mountain biking on gently rolling trails;

horseback riding and kayaking approximately two hours each. No experience necessary.

This program is offered in association with the University of Montana Western, an Elderhostel provider since 1976. Most Elderhostel programs—whether intergenerational or adults only—are offered in conjunction with a local college or university.

AARP Offerings

AARP (American Association of Retired Persons) lists a dozen travel opportunities for grandparents and grandkids. Among these is Thomson Family Adventures—Worldwide Adventures Designed *By* Families *For* Families. This organization has been offering adventure travels for more than twenty years. "We're specialists in exotic and faraway places," reads the brochure. "Our young travelers enjoy discovering the world through guided outdoor adventures, wildlife viewing, cultural exploration, pen pal gatherings and more...courteous guides, travel transfers, delicious meals and comfortable accommodation.... Convenient departures are scheduled to coincide with vacations, and dates are guaranteed, so your trip will not be canceled. What's more, we provide travel insurance at no additional cost."

AARP has a Grandparents' Information Center that offers all kinds of information for grandparents that can be useful whether the grandparent is vacation hosting, visiting grandchildren, or caring for them on a permanent basis. An increasing number of grandparents are assuming the primary role in caring for their grandchildren. The AARP Center offers information and assistance.

Amtrak

Amtrak offers train travel with full accommodations aboard. Its website headlines, "Tired of long lines at the airport? Shocked by outrageous prices at the pumps and sky-high airfares? This year, do something different. Take your vacation by train on Amtrak....

Treat your family to a one-of-a-kind experience. They'll never forget their first trip by train. During the journey, they'll witness an ever-changing panorama unfolding outside the windows.... They may move about the cabin...relax in our spacious seats or drop by the Café Car for a bite to eat, a game of cards, or just to socialize with friends or new acquaintances. In the evening, they enjoy a relaxing meal in the Dining Car.... Over 500 destinations, large and small. It's easy to forget how big and beautiful America is.... Watch the country unfold from comfort in the Sightseer Lounge–Amtrak can take you there."

Listed on the website are destinations such as Washington, D.C., New York City, Orlando, Florida, Seattle, Washington, Boston, Massachusetts, Chicago, Illinois and Portland, Oregon.

Home Depot Offerings

If there's a Home Depot near you, these stores offer Home Depot Kids Clinics. These are how-to clinics for children five to twelve.

Supervision for Underage Children when Traveling Alone

Children are trusting and most look forward to a trip by train, bus, or aircraft with excitement. Each holiday season, thousands head home from school or to visit grandparents or family at a distance from their familiar surroundings—sometimes in a foreign country.

Airlines, Amtrak, and Greyhound Bus Lines have special rules for transporting travelers who are minors. Their lists of restrictions, ages, how to deal with missed connections and supervision, are strict. Parents and grandparents dispatching young children into the wild blue yonder or along the rails or freeways should carefully research these rules and give the children both warnings and how-to instructions.

Amtrak, for instance, allows children fifteen and older to travel unaccompanied, and children eight to fourteen may travel unaccompanied, with certain restrictions.

Continental Airlines does not accept children younger than five years. Unaccompanied minors eight to fourteen are accepted for nonstop direct and connecting flights. Departure and flight times are restricted to daylight hours—except for overnight flights to foreign countries. American Airlines has somewhat different regulations.

Each travel conveyance and company has its own policies and restrictions. All have websites and a number of the well-known ones are listed in the resources section at the back of this book. If you are not familiar with accessing websites, any local library with computer service will have a technician available to help you find the information you need.

In Summary

Grandparents' influence on their grandchildren can be immeasurably great, dismally absent—even dismally present! So much depends on the attitude, the resources, and the time available for all of us. A California license plate frame I saw read: "Only the best Moms become Nanas." This is a tribute to mothers as well as grandmothers, because moms who remember their own loving Nanas are those who pass along that reverence to their children—the grandkids so loved and honored by the grandparents whose information we have quoted or paraphrased.

In addition to the experiences and advice related by the individuals cited in this book, reader parents and grandparents will have suggestions to add. Share your successes and failures with other grandparents struggling to do the right thing by their children and grandchildren, and remember how precious you are to them.

As Grandfather Joseph says, "The whole family, three generations, has always gathered from two states away to attend the annual Los Angeles Auto Show. As soon as I became a grandfather, it was my joyful responsibility to look after the youngest ones. This year I'm grateful at eighty-seven to know they still want to join for the event and the youngest ones are now my guardians and escorts." This is another proof that the investment of love pays lasting dividends—from whatever distance.

Resources

Books

There are plenty of books to help you be an effective long-distance grandparent.

The Don't Sweat Guide for Grandparents: Making the Most of Your Time with Your Grandchildren, by Richard Carlson

Grandloving: Making Memories with Your Grandchildren, 4th Edition, by Sue Johnson and Julie Carlson

Grandparenting From a Distance: An Activities Handbook for Strengthening Long Distance Relationships, The National Institute for Building Long Distance Relationships

Grandparenthood, by Dr. Ruth K. Westheimer

The Grandparent's Guide, by Arthur Kornhaber

How to be the Perfect Grandparent: Rules of the Game, by Bryna Nelson Paston

Little Things Mean a Lot: Creating Happy Memories with Your Grandchildren, by Susan Newman

Totally Cool Grandparenting: A Practical Handbook of Tips, Hints, & Activities for the Modern Grandparent, by Leslie Linsley

Websites

There are quite literally thousands of websites that offer advice and services aimed at making your relationship with your grandchildren more fun and more successful. Here are just a few. Use Google.com to help you find others.

123greetings.com/family/grandchildren —Free e-cards you can send your grandchildren.

Aarp.org/families/grandparents—The American Association of Retired Persons (AARP) website of information for grandparents.

cyberparent.com/gran —Articles, tips, and activities for grandparents.

Flickr.com—This site lets you upload your photos so you can share them with your grandchildren and their parents. Older grandchildren can also put their photos up for you to see.

Forparentsbyparents.com/grandparents_entertain.html—Ideas on how to keep your grandchildren entertained.

Grandparentsmagazine.net —An online magazine just for grandparents.

Photostamps.com—Make actual postage stamps with photos of your grandchildren.

Laterlife.com/laterlife-grandchildren.htm –A U.K. website that lists useful websites and articles for grandparents.

Scrapboook.com –Information and ideas for making scrapbooks. You might make a scrapbook with your grandchild, say of a vacation you took together, or you might make one that shows your grandchild's life.

Raisingyourgrandchildren.com–A website with lots of helpful information for grandparents who are the primary caregiver for their grandchildren.

Travel

There are many places you can take (or meet) your grandchildren, from just the next town over to an exotic foreign country.

Amtrak and each of the airlines have their own policy on children traveling without adult accompaniment, so check first by calling the appropriate reservations department or going to the appropriate website.

Here are some grandparent/grandchild-friendly travel organizations.

Beaches of Turks and Caicos, beaches.com, 1-888-beaches

Educational Odysseys, University of New Hampshire, educationalodysseys.com 887-676-9400

Elderhostel, elderhostel.org, 800-454-5768

Grandtravel, grandtrvl.com 800-247-7651

Great Adventure People, gapadventures.com, 800-708-7761

Rankin Ranch, Rankinranch.com, 661-867-2511

Stanford Family Adventures, stanfordalumni.org, 650-725-1093

Thompson Family Adventures, familyadventures.com, 800-262-6255

Contributors

R.G. Andersen-Wyckoff
Marlene Baird
Don Bauman
Ellen Betts
Phyllis Bufalini
Michelle & Bob Butterworth
Victoria Clark
Ed Clifton
Anne Crosman
Ann Dozier
Lin Ennis
Jane Fisher
Charlotte Foster
Anne & Clark Fowler
Shermane & Larry Frei
Christena Geyer
Alan Gore
Peggy Gorton
Joyce & Mike Heller
Shirley & Joe Hickman
Darlene Holsinger
Leslie Hoy
Joan K. Johnson
Connie Lear
Marjory Lyons
Hope Martinez
Frances McCabe
Nancy McCann
Sue McGinty
Marilyn Meredith
Allison Metzler
Kay Murphy
Judith Naegle

Diane Nielen,
Mindy Nissen
Molly O'Connor
Anne Peterson
Mike Povero
Patti Pruitt
Rita Rainville
Janet & Bill Sabina
Sally & Vic Sanders
Christina & Jim Simpson
John Simpson, Jr.
Elizabeth Singer
Jerry Smith
Sharon & Dale Sutliff
Joe Swavely
Laura Uhlmeyer
Ann Williams
Jacque Winters
Barbara & John Wolcott
Audrey Yanes

Index

About the Author

Willma Willis Gore has been a grandmother for twenty-five years. As a lifelong writer, her byline has appeared on articles, poetry, and short stories in more than eighty national and regional journals. She is the author of *Just Pencil Me In: Your Guide to Moving & Getting Settled After 60*. Gore has been named one of three Accomplished Elders by the Northern Arizona Area Agencies on Aging.

Other Great Books in

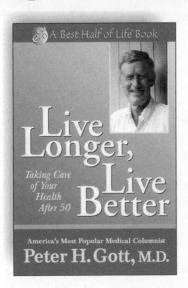

Other Great Books in

The Best Half of Life® Series

Just Pencil Me In
Your Guide to Moving & Getting Settled After 60
by Willma Willis Gore

The first book to address the unique, distinct concerns encountered by those of us over 60 when faced with relocating. Crammed with indispensable tips to make your move uncomplicated and enjoyable.

Videotape Your Memoirs
The Perfect Way to Preserve Your Family's History
by Suzanne Kita and Harriet Kinghorn

Learn how to videotape your life story; the best and easiest way to record your memoirs. This is the first book of it's kind!

The Memory Manual
10 Simple Things You Can Do to Improve Your Memory After *50*
By Betty Fielding

No gimmicks, no long codes or systems to study and memorize, just a simple, holistic program that will get you or a loved one on track to a better memory and a fuller life!